Unbelievably Good Deals & Great Adventures That You Absolutely Can't Get Unless You're Over 50

JOAN RATTNER HEILMAN

CONTEMPORARY
BOOKS

CHICAGO

Library of Congress Cataloging-in-Publication Data

Heilman, Joan Rattner.
    Unbelievably good deals and great adventures that
you absolutely can't get unless you're over 50.

    Includes index.
    1. Travel.   2. Discounts for the aged.   I. Title.
G151.H44   1988   910'.02   88-377
ISBN 0-8092-4320-2

Published by Contemporary Books, Inc.
180 North Michigan Avenue, Chicago, Illinois 60601
Manufactured in the United States of America
Library of Congress Catalog Card Number: 88-377
International Standard Book Number: 0-8092-4064-5

Contents

Chapter One

Introduction to Good Deals and Great Adventures

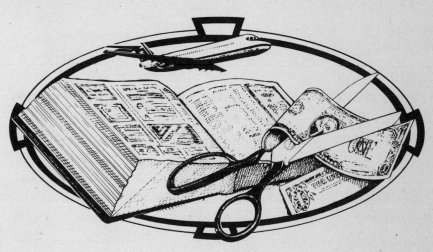

This book is for people who love to do interesting things and go to new places—and don't mind saving money while they're doing it. It is a guide to the perks, privileges, discounts, and special adventures to which you have become entitled simply because you've hung in there for 50 years.

On your 50th birthday, you qualify for hundreds of special opportunities and money-saving offers that will have lots of people wishing they were older. All for a couple of good reasons. First, you deserve them, having successfully negotiated your way through life's white waters. And second, as the fastest-growing segment of the American population, you represent an enormous market of potential consumers, a fact that has become quite apparent to the business community. More than a quarter of the U.S. population today is over 50. One out of every eight Americans is over 65, outnumbering teenagers for the first time in history. Besides, life expectancy is higher today than ever before, and most of us can expect to live a long, healthy, and active life.

Those of us over 50 control most of the nation's wealth, including half of the discretionary income, the money that's left over after essentials have been taken care of, and 80 percent of the savings. For most of us, the children have gone, the mortgage has been paid off, the house is fully furnished, leaving large inheritances is not a major concern, and the freedom years have arrived at last.

As a group, we're markedly different from previous older generations, who pinched pennies and saved them all. We, too, know the value of a dollar, but we feel freer to spend our money because we're better off than our predecessors, a significant number of us having accumulated enough resources to be reasonably secure. We also are far better educated than those before us, and we have developed many more interests and activities.

And, most important, we as a group are remarkably fit, healthy, and energetic. We are in *very* good shape— and feel that way. In fact, a survey has shown that most of us feel at least 15 years younger than our chronological age.

The business community is actively courting "the mature market," as we are known, because now we have the time and the money to do all the things we've always put off. Because of the new recognition of our numbers, our flexible schedules, and our vast buying power, we are finally being taken very seriously. To get our attention, we are increasingly presented with some real breaks and good deals, all of which are detailed on these pages. We are also invited on trips and adventures specifically oriented toward our interests, needs, and abilities. You will find them here too.

In this book, you will learn how to get what's coming to you—the discounts and privileges you couldn't get if you were younger:

▶ The discounts at hotels and motels, at car-rental agencies, on buses, trains, and boats
▶ The best money-saving offers from the airlines that are eager for your patronage
▶ The colleges and universities that offer you an education for free—or nearly
▶ The insurance companies with discounts for people at 50 or thereabouts
▶ The trips, domestic and foreign, designed specifically for the mature market
▶ The free passes to all the national parks
▶ The ski resorts where you can ski for half price—or for nothing
▶ The tennis tournaments, road races, biking events, and beauty contests you may enter
▶ And much more!

Because every community has its own special perks to offer you, make a practice of *asking* if there are breaks to which you are entitled wherever you go, from movies to museums, concerts to historic sites, hotels to ski resorts, restaurants to riverboats, in this country and abroad. Don't expect clerks or ticket agents, tour operators, restaurant hosts, even travel agents to volunteer them to you. First, they may not think of it. Second, they may not realize you have reached the appropriate birthday. Third, they may not want to call attention to your age, just in case that's not something you would appreciate!

Remember to request your privileges *before* you pay or when you order or make reservations, and always carry proof of age or an over-50-club membership card, or, better yet, both. Sometimes the advantages come with membership, but often they are available to anyone over a specified age.

To make sure you're getting a legitimate discount when you want to take advantage of your over-50 privileges, call the hotel, airline, car-rental company, or tour operator and ask what the regular or normal prices are. Then decide whether you are getting a good deal. And, most important, always ask for *the lowest available rate* and compare that to your discounted rate. Frequently you'll find that even better specials are available to you.

With the help of this guidebook, you will have a wonderful time and save money too. Enjoy!

Chapter Two
Travel: Making Your Age Pay Off

P eople over 50 are the most ardent travelers of all. They travel more often, farther, more extravagantly, and for longer periods of time than anybody else. Ever since the travel industry discovered these facts, it's been after our business.

It's fallen in love with our age group because we have more discretionary income than people of other ages. And because we are wonderfully flexible. Many of us no longer have children in school, so we're free to travel at off-peak times or whenever we feel we need a change of scenery. In fact, we much prefer spring and fall to summer. Some of us have retired or have such good jobs that we can make our own schedules. We can even take advantage of midweek slack times when the industry is eager to fill space.

But, best of all, we are energetic, and we're not about to stay home too much. People over 50 account for about one-third of all domestic travel, air trips, hotel/motel nights, and trips to Europe and Africa. Nine out of ten of us are experienced travelers and savvy consumers.

Contrary to what a yuppie might think, people in the over-50 generation aren't content with watching the action; we like to get right into the middle of it. There's not a place we won't go or an activity we won't try. Though many of us prefer escorted tours, almost half of us choose to travel independently.

Not only that, but we're shrewd—we look for the best deals to the best places. We are experienced comparison shoppers and seek the most for our money.

For all these reasons, we are now offered astonishing numbers of travel-related discounts and reduced rates as well as special tour packages and other perks. Many agencies and tour operators have oriented all or part of their trips toward a mature clientele. Others include older travelers with everyone else but offer us special privileges.

Many of the airlines have formed travel "clubs" specifically for older travelers, giving discounts to members who pay a small membership fee to join, or offer passes for a year of travel for one-time payments. Sometimes they give discounts for midweek travel to certain destinations. And most of the hotel and motel chains—as well as individual inns and hotels—now offer similar inducements, such as discounts on rooms and restaurants.

There are so many good deals and great adventures available to you when you are on the move that we'll start right off with travel.

But, first, keep in mind:

▶ Rates, trips, and privileges tend to change at a moment's notice, so check out each of them before you make your plans. Airlines and car-rental agencies are particularly capricious, and it's hard to tell what they offer from one week to the next. The good deals in this guidebook are those that are available as we go to press.

▶ Always ask for your discount when you make your reservations or at the time of purchase, order, or check-in. If you wait until you're checking out or settling your bill, it may be too late.

▶ Also remember that discounts may apply only between certain hours, on certain days of the week, or during specific seasons of the year. Check this out before making reservations and always remind the clerk of the discount when you check in or pay your fare.

▶ It's particularly important when traveling to carry identification with proof of age or membership in an over-50 organization such as AARP or Mature Outlook (see Chapter 19). In most cases, a driver's license or passport does the job. So, in some cases, does the organization's membership card, as well as a birth certificate, a resident alien card, or any other official document showing your date of birth. If you're old enough for a Medicare card or Senior ID card, use that.

▶ Don't always spring for the over-50 discount without checking out other rates. Sometimes special promotional discounts available to anybody any age turn out to be better deals. The railroads, for example, are famous for this. Ask your travel agent or the ticket seller to figure out the *lowest possible available rate* for you at that moment.

▶ If you belong to an organization like AARP or Mature Outlook (see Chapter 19), some of these bargains are yours at age 50. Others come along a little later at varying birthdays, so watch for the cutoff points. Also, in many cases, if the person purchasing the ticket or trip is the right age, the rest of the party or the people sharing the room are entitled to the same reduced rates.

Chapter Three
Out-of-the-Ordinary Escapades

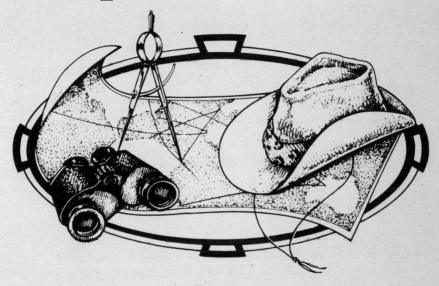

I f you are an intrepid, especially energetic, perhaps even courageous, sort of person who's intrigued by adventures that don't tempt the usual mature traveler, take a look at these possibilities. They are all designed to give you tales with which to regale your friends, relatives, and acquaintances—at least until you embark on the next one!

ALASKA WILDLAND ADVENTURES
See amazing wildlife and spectacular scenery on the Alaska "Senior Safari" offered by Alaska Wildland Adventures, a company that specializes in "soft adventure." You meet in Anchorage for an eight-day trip that starts off with an outdoor salmon bake and includes wildlife tours through national parks and refuges, visits to historic bush towns, a cruise on board a yacht, whale watching, scenic drives, and overnights in comfortable lodges. Except for a few picnics, meals are indoors. The trips, six a season, are limited to 18 participants, and all occur in the summer months.
For information: Alaska Wildland Adventures, PO Box 259, Trout Lake, WA 98650; 1-800-334-8730.

AMERICAN WILDERNESS ADVENTURES

Operated by a nonprofit conservation organization whose main goal is to promote the protection of the environment, these educational walking, backpacking, rafting, and canoeing trips in the wilderness are reserved exclusively for healthy people who are at least 50 years old. In groups of no more than 15 participants led by experienced naturalist guides, you will camp and explore in such places as Canyonlands National Park, Glacier National Park, the San Juan Mountains in Colorado, Yellowstone National Park, the Wind River Range in Wyoming. You may choose to hike on Washington's Olympic Beach and then raft down the Rogue River, walk into extinct volcanoes in Hawaii, or take a canoe trip on the Suwannee River in Florida. No backpacking or mountaineering experience is necessary, but you must have a spirit of adventure!

For information: American Wilderness Adventures of American Wildlands, 7500 E.Arapahoe Rd., Suite 355, Englewood, CA 80112; 1-800-322-WILD.

AMERICAN WILDERNESS EXPERIENCE

If you love roughing it (up to a point) and getting in touch with the earth as it was forever until people began to destroy it in the name of progress, you'll want to consider the trips offered by AWE, which gives discounts to seniors on some of its trips. In addition to horseback, wagon train, llama trekking, canoe, backpacking, fishing, and whitewater rafting adventures, it schedules one trip each year, the Alaska Wildlands Senior Safari, exclusively for the older crowd.

For information: American Wilderness Experience, PO Box 1486, Boulder, CO 80306; 1-800-444-0099 or 303-494-2992.

AMERICAN YOUTH HOSTELS

The outfit that disperses teenagers on low-cost bike trips all over the world is not for youth alone. In fact, it offers an array of inexpensive adventures—bike tours and otherwise—specifically to people over 50. And, of course, older people are invited to go along on any AYH trips labeled "for adults." A recent cycling trip to New Zealand, for example, had an age range of bikers from 23 to 70.

If you want to go on an AYH adventure trip, you must become a member. Membership for adults is $25 a year, unless you've reached 55, in which case you pay only $15. Members get a card and a guidebook that lists hostels in the United States. You may purchase handbooks for Europe and other areas of the world.

The United States affiliate of the International Youth Hostel Federation that coordinates more than 5,300 hostels in 69 countries, the AYH has been operating for over half a century. Each of its trips is limited to 10 participants, including the trip leader. You'll stay primarily in hostels, which are inexpensive dormitory-style accommodations, no two of which are alike. You might stay in a castle in Germany or a lighthouse in California or a budget motel in Massachusetts. Most hostels have kitchens where your group prepares its own meals; a few have cafeterias.

Each year, AYH plans six itineraries for the over-50 crowd, often including hiking or cycling tours, motor trips, and train trips. The recent roster offered a 9-day camping and cycling trip through the cheese country of Wisconsin; another to visit the mountains, glaciers, and lakes of Alaska; two weeks on a mini-van tour through five New England states in the fall foliage season; 9 days of cycling in New England in the fall; 16 days by van in the Pacific Northwest; five weeks by train and ferry through the major countries of Europe; and 16 days by public transportation on an Oktoberfest tour of Bavaria.

In addition to all that, you are entitled to lodge at any youth hostel in the world, including the new network of urban hostels now in Chicago; Washington, D.C.; New York; Boston; San Francisco; Miami Beach; New Orleans; and Los Angeles (one night's stay costs $5 to $20). There is no maximum age limitation for booking a bed in these wonderfully cheap lodgings and hobnobbing with other hostelers who prefer not to pay exorbitant hotel prices. Be ready, however, to sleep in a double-decker cot in a sex-segregated dormitory for about six or eight people supervised by "hostel parents."

For information: American Youth Hostels, Dept. 855, PO Box 37613, Washington, DC 20013-7613; 202-783-6161.

CANADIAN HOSTELLING ASSOCIATION

Canada's hostelling program is similar to that of AYH, although it does not offer adventures designed exclusively for people over 50. Instead, it invites you to join any of its adult trips (here, too, there is no maximum age limit), and hosts Elderhostel Canada programs at some of its more than 70 properties. In addition, as a member, you may lodge at a hostel for $4 to $20 per night, with meals from $2, in Canada—or at any other hostel in the world. Membership for one year costs $18.

For information: Canadian Hostelling Association (L'Association Canadienne de l'Ajisme), 333 River Rd., Vanier, ON K1L 8H9, Canada; 613-748-5638.

MT. ROBSON ADVENTURE HOLIDAYS

For people who love participatory trips, this outfit offers

several adventure vacations every year strictly for people over 50. All of the trips are in Mount Robson Provincial Park, home of the highest mountain in the Canadian Rockies. Golden Week includes two days of hiking, two days of canoeing on spectacular mountain lakes, and a one-day historical tour. You sleep in heated log cabins at the base camp. Or you may choose a five-day heli-camping trip. You are taken by helicopter to a tent camp on the shores of a lake, where you take day trips to points affording spectacular views. Then there are one- to three-day heli-hiking trips for over-50 adventurers. You stay in the base camp's log cabins and are flown off by helicopter to a different mountain area each day.

For information: Mt. Robson Adventure Holidays, PO Box 146, Valemount, BC V0E 2Z0, Canada; 604-566-4351 or 604-566-4386.

OUTWARD BOUND USA

Known for its wilderness-survival trips for youngsters and young adults so they can gain self-confidence and self-esteem and learn to work as a team, Outward Bound has short and popular courses specifically for those at least 50 or sometimes 55. The physical activities are less strenuous than they are for 16-year-olds, but you are expected to push yourself and the goal is the same— to help you discover that there are self-imposed limits, physical and mental, that you can go beyond. Some of the courses have the special goal of helping to effect a smooth transition from career to retirement.

The special four- to nine-day courses for people over 50 include sailing in the Florida Keys (April), sailing off the Maine coast (June or September), canoeing in the lake country of Minnesota (spring), desert backpacking and canyoneering (spring and fall), and mountain expeditioning and canoeing in the Appalachians (fall).

On Outward Bound trips, you live in a tent or under a tarp, sleep in a sleeping bag, cook your own food. You must be in good health although you need not be a veteran athlete.

For information: Outward Bound USA, 384 Field Point Rd., Greenwich, CT 06830; 1-800-243-8520 (in Connecticut, 203-661-0797).

THE OVER THE HILL GANG

The Gang is a club that welcomes fun-loving, adventurous, peppy people over 50 who are looking for action and contemporaries to pursue it with. No naps, no rockers, no sitting by the pool sipping planter's punch. The Over the Hill Gang started as a ski club many years ago but now is into lots of different activities, including travel (see Chapters 13 and 14 for more about the club). Most of the trips are sports-oriented, but some are just plain trips. For example, recent choices have included a Windjammer cruise in the Caribbean; ski trips to Vail, Colorado, Park City, Utah, New Zealand, and the Dolomites in Europe; white-water rafting trips down the Colorado; and a sight-seeing adventure in Switzerland.

You can join one of the many Gangs throughout the country or become a member at large and never lack for company and interesting places to go. Membership in a local Gang is $50 ($80 per couple). If there is no chapter in your area, you may join the national organization for $25 ($40 per couple) and participate in any of the activities.

For information: Over the Hill Gang, 13791 E. Rice Pl., Aurora, CO 80015; 303-699-6404.

GOOD DEAL FOR RVers

International Camper Exchange puts you in touch with people in other countries (notably the UK) who are interested in swapping RVs for a certain period of time, not necessarily simultaneously. When you exchange rigs, you've got a bargain vacation, because no money changes hands and you'll travel rent-free. It takes time to arrange the swap, so sign up many months or even a year before you'd like to travel. You'll receive the names and addresses of one or more interested families, and you take it from there, making your own arrangements. **For information:** International Camper Exchange, 14226 442nd Ave. SE, North Bend, WA 98045.

SENIOR TRAVEL EXCHANGE PROGRAM (STEP)

This is an idea borrowed from student-exchange programs and shares the same purpose of promoting goodwill and world peace, but it's strictly for adventurers over 50. STEP matches you up with foreign hosts in a choice of countries. You stay in their homes, and in return you may wish to play host to overseas visitors who come to see your country. Because you are lodging with families, the cost is very moderate. For example, an 18-day tour of Austria, including air, from New York or California currently costs about $2,000.

Most of STEP's trips are for groups of people staying in different homes for four or five days in each of four communities and include sight-seeing and inland travel with a guide. But you may choose to stay in a home as a single traveler, as a couple, or with a small group of friends, with or without a prearranged itinerary. You must book your trip six months in advance.

STEP, operated by a California nonprofit organization, also offers vacations in low-cost resorts or inexpensive hotels and, where there is no network of host homes, arranges bed-and-breakfast stays for minimal fees.

For information: Send $3 for a brochure with trip details to Senior Travel Exchange Program, PO Box H, Santa Maria, CA 93456; 805-925-5743.

GOING WITH THE GRANDCHILDREN

GRANDTRAVEL

GrandTravel is an innovative vacation program that offers trips for grandparents and their grandchildren so they can share the pleasures of traveling together. "It's a great way to strengthen the link between generations and create lasting memories for everyone," says Helena Koenig, the travel agent who started it. GrandTravel's series of itineraries, scheduled for normal school breaks, aims to appeal to both generations. It includes summer tours to England; trips to Washington, DC, or Alaska; a tour through the American Southwest to learn about Native Americans; African safaris; a visit to Australia; voyages to France or Italy; a tour of western national parks; and barge trips in Holland. GrandTravel will also arrange for independent grandparent/grandchild travel, family groups, or school-sponsored groups.

Actually, you don't have to be a grandparent to take the trips—aunts, uncles, cousins, godparents, and other surrogate grannies are welcome. Ranging from 7 to 17 days, the escorted tours include good hotels with recreation facilities, transportation by motorcoach with rest stops every two hours, and games, talks, and music on the buses. Each trip includes time for the older folks and the children to be alone with their own age group. The kids may go roller skating and dine on fried chicken—supervised, of course—while the grandparents do something grown up, such as going to a gourmet restaurant for dinner.

For information: GrandTravel, The Ticket Counter, 6900 Wisconsin Ave., Chevy Chase, MD 20815; 1-800-247-7651 (in Maryland, 301-986-0790).

GRANDPARENT/GRANDCHILDREN HOLIDAYS

Saga Holidays offers another way for two generations to explore the world together. While you may be any age over 60 (your companion or spouse may be 50 or beyond), the kids must be from 6 to 16. Trips are planned for the Northwest, the national parks, the American Southwest, Disney World, and the California coast—and all during school vacation periods. See Chapter 7 for more about Saga's offerings.

For information: Saga Holidays, 120 Boylston St., Boston, MA 02116; 1-800-343-0273.

THE TRAVELERS' SOCIETY
GRANDPARENT TRIPS

A nonprofit, tax-exempt organization with world peace and understanding of other peoples as its objective, the Travelers' Society offers educational grandparent/grandchildren trips designed, like its other trips, to provide opportunities for two generations of Americans to learn about other societies. Currently, the two-week trips limited to 10 grandparents (or maybe aunts or uncles) and 10 children go to Kenya, where travelers not only see the animals and spend time at the beach but also learn about the African cultures; England and Ireland, where history and current affairs are stressed; and the Soviet Union, where Americans meet Soviets and learn about their common interests.

All contributions and membership fees to the Travelers' Society are tax-deductible as are some travel seminar costs.

For information: The Travelers' Society, PO Box 2846, Loop Station, Minneapolis, MN 55402; 612-342-2788.

R.F.D. TRAVEL

Find new traveling companions: go with your grandkids! With special attractions scheduled along the way for the young folks, this tour operator has put together a couple of trips for the two generations for summer vacation times. The itineraries may vary each year, but recent grandparent/grandchildren adventures have included an American Heritage tour encompassing Washington, DC, Gettysburg, Philadelphia, Williamsburg, and Richmond and a two-week European tour of England, France, Switzerland, the Netherlands, and Germany. Plans are underway for Alaska as well as the Rose Bowl.

For information: R.F.D. Travel, 4801 W. 110th St., Overland Park, KS; 1-800-365-5359.

VISTATOURS

The grandparent/grandchildren tours available from Vistatours are designed to make everybody happy with a wide choice of trips to such places as Washington, DC, and Gettysburg, ranches in Texas, the "wild West," Florida, Mexico, Yellowstone National Park, and Death Valley. The plans include activities for the two generations separately and together, and the goal is for grandparents and grandchildren to become closer through shared experiences.

For information: Vistatours, 1923 N. Carson St., Carson City, NV 89701; 1-800-647-0800.

GRANDPARENTS CAMP
See page 182 for details about a week in the country with your grandchildren during the summer.

Chapter Four

Cutting Your Costs Abroad

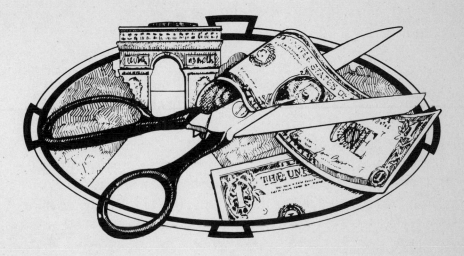

The most enthusiastic voyagers of all age groups, Americans over 50—one out of three adults and a quarter of the total population—spend more time and money on travel than anybody else, especially when it comes to going abroad. It's been estimated that more than 4 out of every 10 passport holders are at least 55 years old. And there's hardly a country in the world today that doesn't actively encourage mature travelers to come for a visit, because everybody has discovered that you are travel's "Now Generation."

Because you are currently being hotly pursued, you can take advantage of many good deals in other lands. This chapter gives you a rundown on ways to cut your European holiday costs, especially if you are planning your trip on your own.

But, first, keep in mind:

▶ Because this is a rapidly changing field as more and more nations and tourist attractions jump on the senior bandwagon, always check the rates as you go. You may find new bargains.

▶ Always have your necessary identification with you (your passport is an excellent ID) and don't be afraid to ask if your age qualifies you for a discount or special fare.

EUROPE BY RAIL

EURAILPASS

To begin with, there is the well-known Eurailpass, valid for unlimited first-class train travel in 17 European countries (including Ireland but not Great Britain). There is no senior discount, but it's certainly worth buying if you plan to cover a lot of miles. Available for various numbers of days up to three months, the passes also get you free or reduced rates on many buses, ferries, and steamers. Traveling with a group of three or more people (or two or more in the off-season) and thereby qualifying for a Eurail Saverpass is especially cheap.

Make sure you buy your Eurailpass before leaving home.

For information: Call your travel agent or write to Eurailpass, Box 325, Old Greenwich, CT 06870.

COUNTRY-BY-COUNTRY TRAVEL DEALS

AUSTRIA

Here a Railways Senior Citizen's ID may be purchased by women over 60 and men over 65 for about $25 at any major railroad station. It is good for a year and may be used to travel anywhere in Austria for half fare on the Austrian Federal Railways and its buses.

For information: Austrian National Tourist Office, 500 Fifth Ave., New York, NY 10036; 1-800-223-0284 or 212-944-6880.

BERMUDA

February is Golden Rendezvous month in Bermuda, a time when special activities, entertainment, and substantial discounts are available to you if you have "a valid senior card." This means you can get these good deals at 50 if you belong to AARP or Mature Outlook, 55 if you don't. Special travel packages are offered by such hotels as Marriott's Castle Harbour Resort, the Elbow Beach Hotel, Mermaid Beach, and Sonesta Beach, among others. For golfers, there's a special tournament for players over 50. A variety of activities are open to you, from walking tours to multimedia shows, sightseeing excursions, and visits to museums and other attractions, most for reduced admission fees. Many of Bermuda's shops will also give you discounts if you flash your identification card.

For information: Call 1-800-223-6106 (in New York, 1-800-223-6107).

FRANCE

The Carte Vermeil for anyone over 60 entitles you to purchase rail tickets within France for half price in either first or second class. Good for a year, it costs 125 francs and may be bought at major railroad stations in France. In general, the 50 percent reduction applies from noon on Saturday until 3:00 P.M. on Sunday and from noon on Monday until 3:00 P.M. on Friday. It is not valid on certain holidays, and you can't buy it in this country.

To get half price on some domestic air flights, movies, museums, and other cultural activities, anyone French or foreign who is 65 need only show proof of age.

For information: French National Railroads, 610 Fifth Ave., New York, NY 10020; 1-800-848-7245.

GREAT BRITAIN

Here's where you're going to get your number-one best bargains in Europe, because the British are really into "the very good years," by which they generally mean over 60. There are discounts and special rates on almost everything—railroads, buses, airlines, canal cruises, many hotels, and just about every historical or tourist site.

The BritRail Senior Pass and the Senior Flexipass (for travelers 60 and over) give you reduced rates on 8-day, 15-day, 22-day, and one-month passes for unlimited travel in England, Scotland, and Wales. They are valid in first class only. The rates are even better than for the regular BritRail Pass, which is a bargain for everyone else. It must be purchased through your travel agent *before* you leave our shores because it is not sold in Britain. By the way, the Eurailpass is not accepted in Great Britain.

In Northern Ireland, you can buy a Rail Runabout ticket at half price.

While people of other ages may need the Britexpress Card, you don't. The card costs $10 and is good for a one-third reduction on the network of routes throughout England, Scotland, and Wales on express buses operated by the National Express Bus Company and Scottish Citylink Coaches. You don't need it because you can automatically get a one-third reduction on any bus fare simply by showing your proof of age.

Be sure to buy a Great British Heritage Pass—again before you leave home—because it gets you admission to more than 600 castles, palaces, and stately homes and gardens in the British Isles, including the Tower of London and Windsor Castle. A 15-day ticket currently costs $39, while a one-month pass is $59.

If you'll be spending much time in London, get the London Visitor Travelcard through your travel agent before you go. With it, you'll get unlimited rides on the city's bus and underground systems as well as tube travel to and from Heathrow Airport. At this writing, the adult pass costs $15 for three days, $21 for four days, and $35 for seven days.

Many theaters offer discounts, although sometimes only for matinees. Check at the box office or ask the hotel concierge.

Hotels also often give senior discounts in the off-season (November through March), so always inquire when you make your reservations. The most notable are the Scottish Highland Hotels, whose Golden Times rates are about a third less all year for anybody over 60 with a minimum stay of two nights. Stakis Hotels, mainly in Scotland, also offer a break—of 10 percent with a two-night minimum stay. Special package holiday breaks are available at certain of these hotels at even cheaper prices. Crest Hotels, a British chain, will give seniors a 15 percent discount at most locations and 10 percent at the others on weekends and midweek Welcome Breaks. And De Vere Hotels offer 15 percent off their basic Leisure Breaks rate at certain hotels. Check these out with your travel agent or with the hotels themselves when you get to the British Isles.

For information: The British Tourist Authority, 40 W. 57th St., New York, NY 10019; 212-581-4700.

GREECE
Here, if you are 60, male or female, you may buy a Hellenic Railways pass that's good for five free single train trips within Greece. When you've used up your five

trips, you may travel on trains and buses at a 50 percent reduction. Valid for one year, the pass may be purchased at any major railroad station in Greece. The only hitch: there are some blackout periods when the card doesn't do the trick. These, of course, probably fall just when you don't want them to—from July 1 to the end of September, plus the 10 days before and after Easter and Christmas.

For information: The Greek National Tourist Organization, 645 Fifth Ave., New York, NY 10022; 212-421-5777.

MAKING FRIENDS BY MAIL

International Pen Friends is a pen-pal organization with more than 160,000 members all over the world. Anybody any age is eligible to join and be matched up with a pen friend in another country—an excellent way to make interesting contacts or practice a foreign language. Membership for one person aged 20 through 59 costs $14; for two people those ages, $20. For one person 60 or over, the membership fee is $10. You will receive a list of 14 names of people in a choice of countries and/or languages who are in your age range and share your interests. (Blind members may request cassette exchanges.)

For information: Send a self-addressed, stamped envelope to International Pen Friends, PO Box 290065, Brooklyn, NY 11229-0001.

ITALY
The Carta d'Argento (Silver Card), which costs a few dollars and is valid for a year, entitles everyone age 60, tourist or resident, to a 30 percent discount on Italian

railways. It can be purchased at railroad stations in Italy at the special windows (Biglietti Speciali) and at C.I.T. offices. Later, flash the card when you buy your tickets.

Note that if you are planning extensive train travel in Italy, however, you may wish to buy a travel-anywhere pass (available to tourists of all ages) called a BLTC, valid for unlimited travel for 8, 15, 21, or 30 days. It's cheap, and it may be a better buy for you. It may be purchased in the United States or in Italy.

For information: Get a BLTC through your travel agent or from Italian State Railways, 666 Fifth Ave., New York, NY 10103; 212-274-0593.

LUXEMBOURG

Anybody over 65 pays half fare on trains and buses. Ask for the discount when you buy your tickets.

For information: The Luxembourg National Tourist Office, 801 Second Ave., New York, NY 10017; 212-370-9850.

THE NETHERLANDS

The Netherlands has no special deals for people over 50, but it does offer a discount card, available to everyone, that's worth considering. It comes in two varieties: The Holland Leisure Card, $12, gives you discounts on hotels, car rentals, trains, domestic air travel, and tourist attractions. The Holland Leisure Card Plus, $30, provides the same benefits but adds the Museum Card, which gets you free admission to over 300 museums. Best to buy your card in the U.S. before you go, by writing to the Board of Tourism.

For information: The Netherlands Board of Tourism, 355 Lexington Ave., New York, NY 10017; 212-370-7367.

SCANDINAVIAN COUNTRIES

If you are 65-plus, you can get around four Scandinavian countries—Denmark, Sweden, Norway, and Finland— by train more cheaply than other adults can.

Denmark gives you half fare outside of peak hours (peak hours are Fridays, 2:00 P.M. to 7:00 P.M.; Saturdays, 8:00 A.M. to noon; Sundays, 2:00 P.M. to midnight) and around the Christmas and Easter holidays.

The Swedish State Railways (SJ) give a 30 percent markdown, with no restrictions on days or times except weekends. The discount also applies on the company's bus routes. In addition, boats and ferries offer special fares, depending on the season.

Norway's offer is 50 percent off the price of a first- or second-class ticket on any train, anytime. To get this, however, you must be 67.

Finland's Senior Citizen Card entitles you to 50 percent off on any train and 30 percent off any bus trip that's at least 47 miles one way—except during weekends and certain holidays.

Note that you should also look into the Scandinavian Bonus Pass. It is not age-oriented but gives discounts off the rates at more than 100 first-class hotels during the summer season in all of these countries plus Iceland.

For a small sum, you can pick up a city card in each capital—Copenhagen Card, Oslo Card, Helsinki Card, Stockholm Card (in Sweden the cards are also available for Gothenburg and Malmo). These cards can simplify your life in these metropolises by giving you unlimited travel on city transportation, free entry to museums and attractions, and discounts on sight-seeing tours, hotels, car rentals, restaurants, events.

For information: The Scandinavian National Tourist Offices, 655 Third Ave., New.York, NY 10017; 212-949-2333.

SWITZERLAND

Switzerland offers some of the best discounts around. As part of its official Season for Seniors, the Swiss Hotel Association provides a list of hundreds of hotels that give reduced rates to women over 62 and men over 65 (if you're a couple, only one of you need be the required age). In most cases, however, you cannot get the discounts during peak holiday seasons, including midsummer.

Note that there are three excellent discount cards available in Switzerland, not just to you but to everyone. One is the inexpensive Swiss Pass that's recommended if you're doing a lot of traveling within the country. The card allows you unlimited travel on the entire network of the Swiss Travel System, including most private and mountain railroads, lake steamers and most postal motorcoaches as well as public tramways and buses in the 24 largest Swiss cities. It also lets you buy excursion tickets to mountaintops at 25 percent off.

The second is the Swiss Half-Fare Card that currently costs 100 Swiss francs (about $65) and is good for a year. Foreign visitors may purchase the half-fare card, valid for one month, for about $45. With the card, you may buy an unlimited number of transportation tickets of all varieties, including excursions to mountaintops, at half price.

The third discount card, the Swiss Card, valid for one month at $80 in first class or $65 in second class (children are cheaper), is good for a round-trip ticket between Zurich or Geneva airports or a Swiss border point and your holiday destination. It also entitles you to buy an unlimited number of transportation tickets at half price on all scheduled services by rail, including mountain railroads, lake steamers, and postal motorcoaches.

For information: Consult your travel agent or the Swiss National Tourist Office in New York (608 Fifth Ave., New York, NY 10020; 212-757-5944) or San Francisco (250 Stockton St., San Francisco, CA 94108; 415-362-2260). In Switzerland, the transport cards are available at railroad stations and airports.

WEST GERMANY

Germanrail's Senioren-Pass offered to everyone over 60 is good for a 50 percent reduction on regular fares in first and second class. It's also valid on some railroads in other countries if you start and finish your trip in Germany. Two varieties are available. Pass A is good only on Mondays, Tuesdays, Wednesdays, Thursdays, and Saturdays. Pass B, more expensive, will do the job every day of the week. Both are valid for a year.

For information: Germanrail, 747 Third Ave., New York, NY 10017; 212-308-3100.

Chapter Five
Trips and Tours for the Mature Traveler

A few sagacious over-50 organizations and travel agencies now cater to "the mature traveler." They choose destinations sure to appeal to those who have already seen much of the world, arrange trips that are leisurely and unhassled, give you like-minded contemporaries to travel with plus group hosts to smooth the way, and provide many services you've decided you're now entitled to. They also give you a choice between strenuous action-filled tours and those that are more relaxed. In fact, most of the agencies offer so many choices that the major problem becomes making a decision about where to go.

Options range from cruises in the Caribbean or the Greek Isles to grand tours of the Orient, sight-seeing excursions in the United States, trips to the Canadian Rockies, theater tours of London, African safaris and snorkeling vacations on the Great Barrier Reef off Australia. There's no place in the world over-50s won't go.

Among the newer and most popular trends are apartment-hotel complexes in American and European resort areas, as well as apartments in major cities. Here you can stay put for as long as you like, using the apartment as a home base for short-range roaming and exploring.

To qualify for most of the trips, one member of the party is supposed to meet the minimum age requirement, and the rest may be younger.

THE OVER-50 CLUBS

AARP TRAVEL SERVICE

AARP (The American Association of Retired Persons) is a huge club (see Chapter 19) that offers all kinds of wonderful benefits, including dozens of trips and tours and discounted cruises, all planned with 50-plus voyagers in mind.

Every season, members get to choose from scores of travel possibilities at enticingly good group rates. There are fully escorted motorcoach tours, deluxe or budget, to Europe, the Soviet Union, Hawaii, Mexico, China, the South Pacific, the United States, and Canada. There are Hosted Holidays in Europe, Mexico, or the Orient, where you will live in an apartment or a hotel, using it as a home base, and exploring the area with the guidance of a local AARP host. Other AARP options include trips to regional celebrations (such as the Mardi Gras in New Orleans) and "independent travel," where you choose lodgings from a selection of AARP-approved properties.

AARP's cruise vacations provide a wide variety of cruise lines with trips to many exotic places, all at substantial savings over regular rates.

If you're a member of AARP, you have already been sent a pile of material about its Travel Service. And you receive its magazine, *Modern Maturity*, which provides ongoing information about the trips and how to sign up for them.

For information: AARP Travel Service, 100 N. Sepulveda Blvd., El Segundo, CA 90245; 1-800-227-7737 from 9:00 A.M. to 5:00 P.M. your time.

MATURE OUTLOOK TRAVEL ALERT
Mature Outlook, the over-50 club run by Sears (see Chapter 19), offers a travel program to its members. This is Travel Alert, which lets you sign up for trips and tours at big savings because they represent unsold space and last-minute cancellations. This means you must be ready to leave with very little notice, maybe a couple of weeks, sometimes less than that. By calling one of a network of participating travel agencies whenever you think you'd like to take off on a trip, you can find out about the currently available trips and the prices.
For information: Mature Outlook, 6001 N. Clark St., Chicago, IL 60660; 1-800-336-6330.

TRAVEL AGENCIES THAT CATER TO OVER-50s

SAGA HOLIDAYS
This 35-year-old British travel firm (in England, people have been known to joke that Saga stands for "Send a Granny Away") specializes in travel for people over 60 (and their spouses or friends over 50). It opened up in the United States and Australia a few years back and is probably now the largest travel company in this field. On its trips, which may be booked only by direct mail or telephone and not through travel agents, Americans find fellow travelers from Great Britain, Australia, and other English-speaking nations. The mix of people from different cultures is an added attraction for many voyagers.
    Once your name is on Saga's mailing list, you will be

faced with constant temptation as the enticing brochures keep on coming. Saga's special features include all-inclusive prices from many departure cities, tour escorts or local guides on call, flight insurance, special Singles Holidays (see Chapter 6) that give you an opportunity to travel with other people who aren't half of a couple, roommate matchups if you want them or, if no roommate is available, only half price on the single supplement.

And more: Grandparents/Grandchildren Holidays (see Chapter 3), free travel if you can gather 20 friends to go on the same trip, and refunds if you must cancel your trip for medical reasons.

It also offers extended stays in apartments or hotels abroad and Add-On Holidays whereby you can tack one trip onto another once you are overseas.

For information: Saga Holidays, 120 Boylston St., Boston, MA 02116; 1-800-343-0273, 9:00 A.M. to 5:30 P.M. EST.

GRAND CIRCLE TRAVEL
Grand Circle caters to people over 50, but if you're a little younger and you really want to go on one of its trips, that's okay too. Founded 30 years ago, this tour operator was the first U.S. company to market senior travel and has escorted more than half a million Americans all over the world.

Grand Circle's trips will take you everywhere, even on an Around the World Tour that stops in "17 exotic destinations" from Katmandu to Nairobi to Beijing. In addition to an endless choice of traditional escorted tours and cruises, this company—which books tours only by mail or telephone—has other intriguing features. For example, it operates a number of apartments and residential hotels around the world, dubbed Extended Vacations for travelers over 50. Your apartment or hotel provides a home base—in such places as London, Italy, Mexico, Spain's Costa del Sol, Yugoslavia, Portugal, Switzerland—for anywhere from 2 to 26 weeks. This way, you can explore at your leisure and perhaps add optional excursions to nearby vacation spots.

And there are other Grand Circle programs. The Countryside Tours, for example, let you stay in destinations that aren't very well known.

As for single travelers, GCT offers a 50 percent discount on the standard hotel and apartment single supplements if you request a travel roommate and none is available for your trip. (See Chapter 6.) On several Extended Vacations, by the way, there are some departure dates with *no* single supplement charge.

For information: Grand Circle Travel, 347 Congress St., Boston, MA 02210; 1-800-248-3737 (in Massachusetts, 1-800-535-8333) Monday through Friday, 8:00 A.M. to 7:00 P.M. EST and Saturday 9:00 A.M. to 5:00 P.M. EST.

GOLDEN AGE TRAVELLERS
This over-50 club specializes in cruises, although it offers other trips as well. When you join the club for $10 a year ($15 per couple), you receive a monthly newsletter with a listing of upcoming adventures, discounts, and bonuses on major cruise lines. Other inducements are tour escorts on every venture and a credit of $15 to $25 per person against the transportation costs to the airport on certain trips. Single travelers may choose to be enrolled in the "Roommates Wanted" list to help find a companion to share the costs.

For members in the San Francisco area, where GAT is

located, there are monthly meetings where you may meet fellow travelers and learn about upcoming trips, limousine service to and from the airport or pier, and one-day mini-tours.

Most of this agency's trips are cruises but cruises everywhere in the world—including the Caribbean, Alaska, the Mediterranean, China and Japan, the South Pacific, between Montreal and New York, and down the Mexican coast and through the Panama Canal and on up the Atlantic coast to Philadelphia. There is also a selection of land tours.

For information: Golden Age Travellers, Pier 27, the Embarcadero, San Francisco, CA 94111; 1-800-258-8880 (in California, 1-800-652-1683).

AJS TRAVEL CONSULTANTS, INC.

The 50 Plus Club, which packages tours for older travelers, is the special concern of AJS Travel Consultants. It markets a series of discounted tours, all leisurely and escorted, ranging from 15 days to 22. Specialties include Switzerland and Italy and especially Israel, where many eventful but relaxed tours are scheduled throughout the year.

For information: AJC Travel Consultants, 177 Beach & 116th St., Rockaway Park, NY 11694; 1-800-221-5002 or 718-945-5900.

MORE, MORE, MORE

ADRIATIC TOURS

All-inclusive senior tours are a specialty of Adriatic Tours, an agency that sends you on off-season (October to April) low-cost holidays in Yugoslavia, sometimes with add-ons to Italy and the Soviet Union. Most trips are for

two weeks, but you may stay longer at very little cost per week or add mini-vacations to Athens, Budapest, Istanbul, or Rome.
For information: Call your travel agent or contact Adriatic Tours, 691 W. 10th St., San Pedro, CA 90731.

BACK-ROAD TOURING CO.

Designed especially for adults over 50, the tours planned by this agency take small groups (no more than 12 at a time) through the British Isles along the back roads to out-of-the-way places. You travel with a guide for two weeks by minivan, stay in inns, historic houses, farms, and bed-and-breakfasts, and don't spend a fortune. If you organize your own group of eight travelers, you and a companion get to travel free.
For information: Back-Road Touring Co., c/o Chusa, Inc., 242 Bellevue Ave., Upper Montclair, NJ 07043; 1-800-526-2915 or, in New Jersey, 201-744-8724.

BONANZA HOLIDAYS

The winter long-stay holidays offered by Bonanza's Club 50 from mid-January through March take you, inexpensively, via Air Canada to such places as Spain's Costa del Sol, Portugal's Algarve, Tunisia, Hawaii, Egypt, southern California, or Turkey. There you settle in for three weeks or so, taking side trips as you like. All departures are from Toronto, with nominal add-on fares for those from other locations. Most overseas holidays include a few nights in London.
For information: Call your travel agent or contact Bonanza Holidays, 310 N. Queen St., Suite 201 N., Etobicoke, ON M9C 5K4, Canada.

CHOOSING A PLACE
TO SETTLE DOWN

Lifestyle Explorations conducts group two-week tours of several parts of the world that it considers to be "ideal retirement communities." You'll tour areas of Costa Rica, or the Algarve in Portugal, or Uruguay and Argentina, and attend a series of seminars and meetings with local authorities in the medical, legal, business, investment, and real-estate fields. You'll have conversations and meals with Americans already living there as well as sightseeing adventures. In this way, says Jane Parker, a retirement planning counselor who runs this tour agency, you can find out first-hand what it's like to live in these foreign lands before you make any hard decisions. All of these places were chosen and rated according to cost of living, taxes, health care, climate, safety, friendliness of the people, government stability, and cultural opportunities.

For information: Lifestyle Explorations, PO Box 57-6487, Modesto, CA 95355; 209-577-4081.

CANNON TOURS & TRAVEL

The 50's Plus program of Cannon Tours, a Canadian tour operator headquartered in Toronto, specializes in three categories of inexpensive holidays for the older crowd. Its "Go-Go" tours are designed for energetic folks who can tolerate long flights and full sight-seeing days (for example, tours of the Soviet Union and the South Pacific). "Slow-Go" trips, perhaps to the Canadian West and the Rockies, or California and Arizona, spend a few nights in each place and limit the length of the driving from hither to yon. "No-Go" are stays all in one place, such as St. Petersburg, Scottsdale, or Victoria, British Columbia.

For information: Call your travel agent or contact Cannon Tours & Travel, 234 Eglinton Ave. East, Toronto, ON M4P 1K5, Canada; 416-481-6177.

LOVE HOLIDAYS

For the "mature sophisticated traveler," Love Holidays features trips to the resorts and major cities of Yugoslavia with side adventures to other parts of Eastern Europe, including Austria, Hungary, Greece, Romania, Turkey, and the Soviet Union. Its all-inclusive packages are escorted and inexpensive because of its group rates.
For information: Call your travel agent or contact Love Holidays, 15315 Magnolia Blvd., Sherman Oaks, CA 91403; 1-800-456-5683 or, in the Los Angeles area, 213-873-7991.

MAYFLOWER TOURS

Mayflower plans trips for people "55 or better." Most departures are from Chicago with overnight accommodations arranged for travelers from surrounding states. Some of the agency's more far-flung tours, however, leave from other cities. All trips are fully escorted by tour directors whose job it is to make sure all goes well and everybody has fun. The pace is leisurely, and rest stops are scheduled for every couple of hours. You travel by air-conditioned motorcoach, stay in quality hotels or motels, and eat most of your meals together.

If you are a single traveler and make your trip reservation at least 30 days before departure, you'll get a roommate or travel at the regular double rate.

All of the agency's trips are within the United States (Hawaii included), with tours, for example, through the

Canadian Rockies, Florida, California, or Georgia's Golden Isles.

For information: Call your travel agent or contact Mayflower Tours, 1225 Warren Ave., Downers Grove, IL 60515; 1-800-323-7604 or 708-960-3430.

SCI/NATIONAL RETIREES OF AMERICA

This agency, which began 30 years ago with trips to the Catskill resorts, now has a long list of group tours for seniors that range from one-day outings to 12-day cruises. The tours are all in the Northeast, depart midweek, and transport you by motorcoach. Choices of destination are myriad.

For information: SCI/National Retirees of America, 134 N. Franklin St., Hempstead, NY 11550; 1-800-645-3382 or, in New York, 516-481-3939.

SENIOR ESCORTED TOURS

Specializing in vacations in Cape May, a beautiful little coastal town at the southern tip of New Jersey that abounds in Victoriana, this company also offers package trips to such places as Orlando, Florida, Boston, Nova Scotia, Cape Cod, and the Catskills in New York—most of them including all meals. There are Caribbean and Alaskan cruises, as well as adventures in Australia, Hawaii, and the U.S. national parks.

For information: Call your travel agent or contact Senior Escorted Tours, PO Box 400, Cape May Court House, NJ 08210; 1-800-222-1254.

RETIRING IN MEXICO

Retire in Mexico (RIM), a travel company based in California, has organized a series of seminars and educational tours for people who are thinking about the possibility of retiring in Mexico, a neighboring country where the American dollar currently goes very far. Could Mexico provide a happy home for you? You can find out by attending seminars given periodically in a number of cities in the United States, and then, if the idea intrigues you, signing on for a group visit to one or more of about a dozen south-of-the-border areas. You travel around the town and countryside by car or van with a small number of other potential retirees, and attend lectures on such subjects as health facilities, housing, investments, Mexican culture, and immigration.

On a typical tour, for example, you would spend three nights in Mexico City, then two each in San Miguel de Allende, Guanajuato, Morelia, and three in Guadalajara. There are other choices as well, all places with significant North American populations. In each area, you get conferences and tours conducted in English. (Point of information: Mexicana Airlines gives 10 percent discounts, in off-peak seasons, to travelers over 62 and their any-age companions on flights between Mexico and many U.S. gateway cities. See Chapter 7.)

For information: Barvi Tours, 11658 Gateway Blvd., Los Angeles, CA 90064; 1-800-824-7102 (in California, 213-475-1861).

YUGOTOURS

It may not come as a surprise that Yugotours, owned by the Yugoslavian government, features trips to Yugoslavia. It has become known for its "Prime of Your Life Vacations" for anybody who is retired or over 60 (plus companions of any age). Offered all year round, the vacations take you via Yugoslav Airlines to your pick of resorts in Yugoslavia on the coast, at inland lakes, or in the mountains, depending upon the season. Rates vary according to the time of year but are all-inclusive and very reasonable.

On this venture, you can customize your trip to suit yourself, taking it slow or becoming involved in the activities organized by the tour director in your hotel. You may spend your entire vacation in one resort, or in a combination of places, and you may stay as many weeks as you like. Included in the package are breakfast and dinner.

While you're there, you may avail yourself of special mini-holidays—three nights in a choice of cities in nearby countries, such as Rome, Athens, Budapest, Istanbul, or Prague. And, at the end of your stay, you have the option of prolonging your trip with special extensions, such as a week in the Soviet Union, a tour of the Dalmatian Coast, or a cruise on the Adriatic Sea.

For information: Call your travel agent or contact Yugotours, 350 Fifth Ave., New York, NY 10118; 1-800-223-5298 (in New York State, 212-563-2400).

CRUISING THE HIGH SEAS

Cruises have always appealed to the mature crowd. In fact, most sailings abound with people who are at least a few decades out of college. So, whatever trip you choose, you are sure to find suitable companionship. However, there are some special deals designed especially for you.

PREMIER CRUISE LINES
Combine four-night cruises to the Bahamas out of Port

Canaveral, Florida with three days in Disney World, and, if you are over 59, get a 10 percent discount. Anybody else who shares your cabin gets the discount, too. Although the savings can't be combined with other promotional rates, it can be added to the advantages you earn by booking early (upgrades in cabin category).

Here's what you get: A four-night cruise to Nassau and Salt Cay in the Bahamas, then three nights in a hotel near Disney World, free admission to Disney's Magic Kingdom and Epcot Center, as well as Spaceport, USA, plus a rental car with unlimited mileage thrown in.

For information: Call your travel agent, or contact Premier Cruise Lines, PO Box 573, Cape Canaveral, FL 32920; 1-800-327-7113 (in Florida, 305-783-5061).

SEA ESCAPE CRUISE LINES

If you're spending time in Florida and you have passed your 55th birthday, you may want to take advantage of the discounts on the one-day cruises run by this line. You can get a senior discount anytime during the year, but you'll get your best savings from April 1 to June 30, every day but Saturday. These short cruises leave from Miami, Fort Lauderdale, St. Petersburg, and Port Canaveral.

For information: Call 1-800-327-7400 (in Florida, 1-800-432-0900).

SINGLEWORLD

Singleworld caters to people "over 35" who like to cruise the seas and spend time ashore sight-seeing, shopping, and sunning. Using major cruise lines and charging fares that are usually well below the regular tariffs, Singleworld schedules its trips at nonpeak times—commonly in fall and early winter. At this moment, destinations include Caribbean ports as well as Cancùn and Cozumel in Mexico, and cruises to the Far East.

Cruise passengers are guaranteed lower berths, the first sitting in the dining room, exclusive shore excursions, and special activities such as cocktail parties just for your crowd.

A special escort is sent along on every cruise to organize shipboard activities and shore excursions and, in general, to make sure all goes well.

Accommodations for solo travelers are arranged on a shared basis, meaning that you'll be assigned a suitable roommate if you haven't brought your own.

For information: Call your travel agent or contact Singleworld, PO Box 1999, Rye, NY 10580; 1-800-223-6490 or 914-967-3334.

SOUTH FLORIDA CRUISES

This cruise clearinghouse specializes in bargain trips to the Caribbean, Mexico, South America, the Panama Canal, Europe, Alaska, the South Pacific, and the Far East, giving passengers substantially reduced rates. Its method is to purchase large blocks of space on brand-name cruise lines and pass some of the savings along. What's more, it has declared it will give you an *additional* discount of about $50 per cabin if you are over 50 years of age and mention the "Unbelievably Good Deals and Great Adventures Special." In other words, say you found this information in this book!

For information: South Florida Cruises, Inc., 2005 Cypress Creek Rd., Fort Lauderdale, FL 33309; 1-800-327-SHIP (in Florida, 305-493-6300).

SIGHT-SEEING BY RAIL

Traveling by rail is a comfortable way to see the country, more leisurely than flying and more spacious than going by bus. But we know of only one tour operator offering a special deal to mature travelers.

OMNI SENIOR RAIL TOURS

You can tour the United States by rail at group rates with Omni Senior Rail Tours, an agency that runs many trips originating in Chicago for people over 50. You'll go by Amtrak and, where airline service is required, United Airlines. For local sight-seeing excursions, you'll travel by motorcoach. The tours of about 35 people are escorted and include transportation, hotels, many meals, sight-seeing trips, and entertainment. If you start from a city other than Chicago, you will be met in the Windy City, or you may join the tours along the way.

The itineraries include travel to Florida; Texas; the Pacific Northwest; California; the national parks; Las Vegas, Reno, and Lake Tahoe; the Atlantic Northeast and Canada for a fall foliage tour; and a tour of the "Romantic South," meaning Natchez and New Orleans. You'll see all the major sights in these areas.

For information: Call your travel agent or contact OmniTours, 1 Northfield Plaza, Northfield, IL 60093; 1-800-962-0060.

SPECIAL TRIPS TO ISRAEL

Israel is a favorite travel destination for many over-50 travelers, so several tour operators and Jewish organizations have designed visits especially for them. The trips are usually at least three weeks long and organized in a leisurely fashion with plenty of free time.

AMERICAN JEWISH CONGRESS

The AJC runs lots of trips everywhere from the Caribbean to India, but specializes in Israel. Its longer trips, usually 22 or 27 days, are designed especially for people with plenty of time for an easygoing itinerary and so tend to appeal to older travelers. Traveling alone? You may want to choose AJC's special singles trips. There are two departures a year for singles between the ages of 39 and 55 and four a year for single adventurers over the age of 55.

For information: American Jewish Congress, 15 E. 84th St., New York, NY 10028; 1-800-221-4694 (in New York State, 212-879-4588, 516-752-1186, or 914-328-0018).

EL AL

The Israeli airline not only flies (at 60, you'll get a 15 percent discount off airfares; see page 81) but also packages trips. Its 22-day Israel at Leisure Tours for people over 50 spend time in Tel Aviv, Jerusalem, and the Galilee, all with English-speaking guides.

The Jewish Heritage Tours—one to eastern Europe (Prague and Budapest) and Israel and another to Spain and Israel—are designed to give American Jews an opportunity to explore their roots and are planned with older travelers in mind.

For information: Call your travel agent or contact El Al, 850 Third Ave., New York, NY 10022; 1-800-352-5786 or, in New York, 212-768-9200.

NATIONAL COUNCIL OF YOUNG ISRAEL

Once a year, the Senior League of this organization

offers a three-week tour of the country, a package deal that includes everything.

For information: National Council of Young Israel, 3 W. 16th St., New York, NY 10011; 212-929-1525.

Chapter Six
Singles on the Road

Lots of over-50s love to travel but don't have anybody to do it with. If you're single, single once again, or have a spouse who isn't the traveling kind, there's no need to give up your dreams of faraway places simply because you don't want to travel alone. There are many organizations and packagers ready to come to your aid. Some offer special trips for mature singles where you mingle with others on their own, and many help match you up with a fellow traveler who is also looking for a compatible person with whom to share adventures, a room, and expenses. Traveling with another person is usually more fun and certainly less expensive than going alone because you share double accommodations, thereby avoiding the single supplement, which can be substantial.

MATCHMAKERS

TRAVEL COMPANION EXCHANGE
Specializing in finding the right travel companion from all age groups from 18 to 85, TCE matches up single, divorced, or widowed travelers for joint adventures. Operated by travel expert Jens Jurgen, who is always

thinking up new ways to matchmake and make traveling more fun, this organization, the largest and most enduring of its kind, works hard at making compatible connections and has been very successful. Members—who pay $66 for six months—receive chatty bimonthly newsletters stuffed with travel tips and frequent listings of people actively seeking travel partners. For more details on those who seem good possibilities, you send for Profile Pages—or others send for yours—so that you may judge suitability for yourself. You do your own matchmaking. Mr. Jurgen suggests you talk by telephone, correspond, meet, and, even better, take a short trip together before setting out on a major adventure. By the way, TCE gives free membership to unmarried older men!

For information: Travel Companion Exchange Inc., PO Box 833, Amityville, NY 11701; 516-454-0880.

GOLDEN COMPANIONS

Exclusively for travelers over 49, Golden Companions will help you find company to wander with, perhaps another solo voyager or a small group that moves out together. "It is for those who do not want to travel alone, for those who do not want to travel in large groups, and for those wishing to expand their existing circle of travel friends," says Joanne Buteau, its founder. A six-month membership at this writing costs $48, which entitles you to a newsletter, the networking service, a mailing list, and a mail-exchange service. This club gets you discounts on some tours for mature travelers and organizes its own cruises and tours for its members. Upcoming trips include cruises in Alaska and the Caribbean.

For information: Golden Companions, PO Box 754, Pullman, WA 99163; 509-334-9351.

PARTNERS-IN-TRAVEL

This group is devoted to making travel a happier experience for solo travelers through contacts and connections. With a newsletter and its Match Up service, the goal is to link up travel companions, most of them in the "mature" category. The newsletter prints mini-listings that will be followed up, upon request, by more detailed profiles of members seeking travel companions. Membership currently costs $45 per year. An additional service is a Vacation Home Exchange program available to members who wish to extend hospitality and/or accommodations to fellow members.

For information: Partners-in-Travel, PO Box 491145, Los Angeles, CA 90049; 213-476-4869.

TOURS FOR SOLO TRAVELERS

Several tour operators and agencies specializing in escorted trips for people in their prime will try to find you a roommate (of the same sex) to share your room or cabin so you will not have to pay a supplement. And, if they can't manage to find a suitable roommate, they will usually reduce the supplement even though you'll have your own private room. Some run singles trips as well. In any case, keep in mind that you'll hardly have time or opportunity to be lonely on the typical escorted tour run by these agencies. If you are planning an extended stay in one place, however, you may have more need for company.

For more about the tour operators listed below, see Chapter 5. Other companies may offer the same singles-matching service, though they don't make a point of it, so always ask about it if you're interested.

AMERICAN JEWISH CONGRESS

Singles who would like to travel to Israel or other international destinations with a group of solo travelers in their own age range should check out the trips run by the American Jewish Congress. There are trips every year for singles aged 35 to 55 and several for singles over 55. The age requirements are not ironbound—you choose the group with which you feel most comfortable. If you ask AJC to find you a roommate, and it can't, it guarantees a single room without the single supplement.

For information: American Jewish Congress, 15 E. 84th St., New York, NY 10028; 1-800-221-4694 (in New York state, 212-879-4588; 516-752-1186; 914-328-0018).

CLASSIC SINGLES NETWORK

If you want to avoid the possibility of being a single person on a tour filled with couples and would prefer traveling with other "mature singles," check this agency out. Part of Olson Travel, it offers escorted packaged tours for small groups of older solo travelers to many parts of the world that currently include Italy, France, the Orient, Hawaii, and Egypt. Hotels are first class or deluxe, you share a twin room, and breakfast and some other meals are included. Several tours are offered for holiday seasons—around Thanksgiving and Christmas— when many older singles like to be on the move.

For information: Call your travel agent or 1-800-421-2255 or, in California, 1-800-421-5785.

GOLDEN AGE TRAVELLERS

An over-50 club, Golden Age Travellers will enroll you in its "Roommates Wanted" list if you wish help in finding a companion with whom to share the costs and the fun. **For information:** Golden Age Travellers, Pier 27, The Embarcadero, San Francisco, CA 94111; 1-800-258-8880 (in California, 1-800-652-1683).

GRAND CIRCLE TRAVEL

Grand Circle, which concentrates on over-50 travel packages, tries to match singles with appropriate roommates if they request them. If there are none at hand, you will be charged only half the single supplement for your own room. And on several of its Live Abroad Vacations departure dates, you will not pay a single supplement at all.

This company also offers special singles departure dates, with 50 percent off the standard hotel and apartment single supplements. Plus, its newsletter has a Pen Pal section that allows members of GCT's Travel Club to make new friends and perhaps find people to travel with. **For information:** Grand Circle Travel, 347 Congress St., Boston, MA 02210; 1-800-248-3737 (in Massachusetts, 1-800-535-8333).

MAYFLOWER TOURS

Another travel operator with mature travelers as its focus, Mayflower also gets you a roommate or, if that's not possible, charges you only the regular double rate without the single supplement. Its Serendipity Club in Chicago provides an additional way to match yourself up with a potential traveling companion. **For information:** Mayflower Tours, 1225 Warren Ave., Downers Grove, IL 60515; 1-800-323-7604 or 708-960-3430.

SAGA HOLIDAYS

A tour company specializing in trips for people over 60 (see Chapter 5), Saga Holidays will try to find a roommate for you on its escorted tours. If there is none to be found, you will be charged only half the single supplement. Its Penfriends and Partnerships program prints "personals" in its newsletter so members may meet each other by mail and perhaps find a travel partner in the bargain. This company also schedules several exclusive Singles Departures, usually to destinations within the United States, each season. On these, the single supplement prices are reduced and you are guaranteed a roommate if you want one, or you will get your own room at the twin-share price.

For information: Saga Holidays, 120 Boylston St., Boston, MA 02116; 1-800-343-0273.

SINGLEWORLD

To help you enjoy vacationing in the company of others, while avoiding single-supplement fees, Singleworld offers its members cruises and tours specifically for solo travelers. Members, who pay a membership fee of $25 a year, also receive a quarterly newsletter. You will fit best into Singleworld's trips "for over-35" or "all ages," categories that attract the over-50s.

For information: Singleworld, P.O. Box 1999, Rye, NY 10580; 1-800-223-6490 or 914-967-3334.

SOLO FLIGHTS

This travel agency arranges vacations specifically for single travelers of all ages, with much of its clientele on the far side of 50. It keeps track of the best tours, cruises, packages, groups, and rates for single people, and so with one telephone call or a letter you can find out—at no charge—what's out there that interests you, from weekend getaways to full-length vacations offered by major tour operators, including Club Med, as well as lesser-known possibilities. Of course, the agency will do your booking.

For information: Solo Flights, 127 S. Compo Rd., Westport, CT 06880; 203-226-9993.

DANCE CRUISES

Designed for women from 50 to 90 who love to dance but don't have partners, the Merry Widows Dance Cruises runs several cruises every year to such places as the Caribbean, the Orient, Alaska, Greece and the Mediterranean, and the South Pacific. The trips range from seven days to 18. Under the auspices of the Tampa AAA (American Automobile Club), the cruises take along one male professional dance teacher for every five women on the trip. Each woman receives a dance card that rotates her partners every night throughout the cruise, whether she's a beginner or a polished dancer. The men are also rotated at the dinner tables so everyone gets the pleasure of their (platonic) company. You don't have to be a widow and you don't even have to know the cha-cha to have fun on these trips.

For information: Call your travel agent or contact Merry Widows Dance Cruises, PO Box 31087, Tampa, FL 33622; 813-289-5923.

SUDDENLY SINGLE TOURS
This agency offers first-class-all-the-way group tours in this country and abroad exclusively for people "over 40"

who have suddenly become single again in midlife. Its travel programs "are designed with your maturity, tastes, and needs in mind." Departures are from the Midwest and New York. The guided trips, both in this country and in foreign lands, are designed to provide deluxe accommodations and private rooms for everyone. **For information:** Suddenly Single Tours, Ltd., 161 Dreiser Loop, New York, NY 10475; 212-379-8800.

HOOK-UPS FOR LONE RVers

RVers who travel alone in their motor homes or vans can hook up with others in the same circumstances when they join one of the groups mentioned below. Both provide opportunities to travel together or to meet at campgrounds on the road, making friends with fellow travelers, and having fun.

LONERS OF AMERICA

LOA stresses that it is not a matchmaking organization but rather a club for single RVers who want to travel together. In existence only a few years, it now has 29 chapters throughout the country and 1,400 members from their 40s to their 90s, almost all retired and all widowed, divorced, or otherwise single. Many of them live year-round in their motor homes or vans, and others hit the road only occasionally. They camp together, rally together, caravan together, often meeting at special campgrounds that cater to solo RVers.

A not-for-profit member-operated organization, the club sends you an annual membership directory and a lively bimonthly newsletter that lets you know about campouts and rallies all over the country. The chapters organize their own events as well. Dues are $20 a year plus a $5 registration fee for new members.

For information: Loners of America, Rte. 2, Box 85E, Ellsinore, MO 63937; 314-322-5548.

LONERS ON WHEELS

Most of the members of Loners on Wheels, a 54-chapter national recreational club, are retired and over 50, but the only ironclad rule for membership is that you are single! "There are literally hundreds of campouts each year sponsored by the chapters, as well as about 12 large rallies each year in various parts of the country and Canada," according to its literature. All kinds of RVs are included, as well as all kinds of people who participate in all kinds of recreational and educational activities. Aside from the outings, there are Loners on Wheels campgrounds in the Ozarks, Florida, and California.

For information: Write to Loners on Wheels, PO Box 1355, Poplar Bluff, MO 63901; 314-785-2420.

Chapter Seven
Airfares: Improving with Age

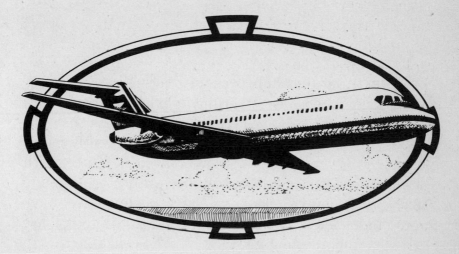

One thing that improves with age—yours—is air-fare. Almost every airline in existence now offers discounted senior fares and sometimes they are the best deals around. The airlines are currently using four ways of attracting mellow travelers: clubs with discounts, discounts without clubs, unlimited-mileage passes, and coupon books. That's because we have proved to be the hottest travel market to tap today. We are a vast and growing group of careful consumers with money in our pockets and time on our hands during slack off-peak periods, just when the airlines like to fill up seats.

The minimum age for senior fares is 50, but most of the discounts are offered later—when you are 60 or 62 or 65. Most programs allow a companion of any age, regardless of sex or relationship, to travel with you at the same reduced fare, although occasionally that person must pay a fee for the privilege. In some cases, however, your younger companion must be married to you to get the slashed prices.

Several airlines have arrangements with car-rental companies and hotel chains to provide discounts on these, too. (See Chapter 8 for more on car rentals and Chapter 10 for more on hotels and motels.)

But, first, keep in mind:

▶ Always ask your travel agent or the airline reservations clerk to get you the *lowest possible fare*. Mention the fact that you qualify for a senior discount, but be prepared to jump ship if you can get a better deal by going with a special promotional rate or a super super-saver fare—although sometimes your discount can cut these lowest fares even lower. Many airlines now offer special promotional fares for seniors during off-peak seasons. Watch for these sales; they are usually the cheapest way to go, especially when you can deduct the airline's regular senior discount from them.

▶ Keep in mind that the restrictions you must fly by may not be worth the savings. Always examine the fees and conditions and decide whether you can live with them. There may be blackout periods around major holidays when you can't use your discount, departures only on certain days or hours, restrictions on the season of the year, or stiff penalties for flight changes. In some plans, you must travel the entire distance on one airline even if connections are poor. It's not easy to sort out the offers because some carriers give better discounts but more hassles—or vice versa—so make comparisons before arriving at a decision.

▶ Before you decide to buy a yearly pass or a coupon book, figure out how many trips you're likely to make during the next year. Unless you see clear savings, you are better off with individual tickets. But if you travel frequently, or would do so once you had the pass, then it could be an excellent buy.

▶ Book your flights as early as possible for the best fares and the most available seats (frequently, the number of seats is severely limited). Try to couple your senior discounts with ultimate supersaver fares, which require 30-day advance purchase and include other restrictions on length of stay, and days on which you may fly.

▶ Be prepared to present a membership card (if you are flying as a member of a club) and a valid proof of age at the check-in counter. It's possible that your discount will not be honored if you don't have that proof with you, and you will have to pay the difference.

Now for some of the potential bargain offers. Be advised that airfares and airline policies often change overnight, so call the airline that interests you for an update.

U.S. SKIES: MAJOR AIRLINES

AMERICAN AIRLINES

AA's Senior Discount entitles anyone 62 or over to a 10 percent discount off all fares, one way or round-trip, simply for the asking. And it gives the same savings to a traveling companion who may be too young to get his or her own discount. Frequent-flyer points are yours, too.

If you are a member of AARP, you can get 10 percent off when you're only 50 years old. You and your member spouse, whatever age, get the reduced rate on the lowest coach excursion fares. However, the AARP discount applies to round-trip tickets only. Also, you must buy your tickets at least 30 days in advance (it's suggested you make your purchase even earlier, because seats are limited) and plan to stay over a Saturday night. There is a 50 percent penalty for cancellations or change of itinerary, and there are certain holiday blackout periods. Yes, you're entitled to frequent-flyer credits when you fly with this discount. And 10 percent off on Avis car rentals too.

American Airlines offers another good deal if you are 62 and travel enough in a year's time to make it worthwhile. That's its Senior TrAAveler Coupon Books. For $420 ($105 per one-way trip) you may buy a four-coupon book, and for $704 ($88 per trip) you may buy an eight-coupon book. Each coupon is good for travel one way up to 2,000 miles in the 48 contiguous states as well as Hawaii and Puerto Rico. (That means a flight from New York to California, for example, would cost you more than one coupon.) You may travel any day of the week, but you must buy your tickets at least 14 days in advance. There is no refund on the coupons and no change of itinerary once you exchange a coupon for your ticket. Seats are limited, and there are some blackout periods on peak travel days during holiday times. You'll get frequent-flyer credits for these flights, however.

American Eagle, a commuter airline, is part of American Airlines, and the privileges above apply to its flights.

For information: Call your travel agent or 1-800-433-7300 for reservations or Senior Discounts. For the Senior TrAAveler Coupon Books, call 1-800-237-7981.

CONTINENTAL

You, and a travel mate of any age, will get a flat 10 percent discount on Continental Airlines on all fares, even the lowest, if you are 62. Just ask for it and be ready to prove your age. You'll be eligible for frequent-flyer credits with these tickets.

Or, if you do a lot of traveling, consider the Freedom Passport. This gives you virtually unlimited travel for a year in the United States for $1,599 coach or $1,999 first class as we go to press (renewals are cheaper). Options allow you to add on trips to Mexico, the Caribbean, or Central America for $150 each, Hawaii for $300, Europe for $400, or the South Pacific for $500. If you'd rather be eligible to fly all over the world, including the United States, on your passport, buy the global version for $2,999 coach, $4,999 first-class (again, renewals cost less).

Some restrictions: You may fly to the same city only three times during the year. Seats are limited, and there are some blackout periods around major holidays. You are entitled to one one-way trip per week and must stay over a Saturday night. For domestic flights travel is restricted to noon Monday through noon Thursday and all day Saturday, and reservations may be made no earlier than seven days in advance. For international flights, hours are all day Monday through Thursday and Saturday, and reservations can be made no earlier than 21 days in advance. No frequent-flyer credits are given for tickets purchased with the passport. However, a Companion Passport is also available for the same price for your travel mate, who may be younger but must always be the same person.

For information: Call your travel agent or 1-800-525-0280 for reservations or 1-800-441-1135 for the Freedom Passport.

DELTA

If you are over 62, you get a 10 percent reduction on the lowest available fare, and so does your traveling companion of any age. You also get frequent-flyer credits.

Delta's other good deal, its Young at Heart Coupon Program for travelers over 62, gives you a book of coupons good for one-way travel at low prices if you use them all within a year. It currently costs $420 ($105 per trip) for four coupons and $704 ($88 per trip) for eight coupons. One coupon will take you anywhere the airline flies in the continental United States and Puerto Rico; two coupons are required to fly to Alaska or Hawaii. You may fly any day of the week, but seats are limited, so book ahead. Tickets must be validated at least 14 days in advance of your flight. You'll get frequent-flyer credits for the miles you fly.

For information: Call your travel agent or 1-800-221-1212.

EASTERN

Eastern, still flying at press time, offers a few excellent choices to older travelers. The first is its Get Up and Go Passport that saves money for people over 62 who plan a lot of trips. For the current price of $1,199 you may make one trip per week within a year to more than 100 destinations in the United States, Canada, the Virgin Islands, and Puerto Rico. You may buy a second passport for a traveling companion, any age, at the same price. For $1,599 you may make the flights first class. You'll get no frequent-flyer credits for passport flights.

Among the restrictions: You may fly only from noon Monday through noon Thursday and all day Saturday. There are blackout periods during major holidays. Seats are limited. You are entitled to no more than three flights to the same city during the year.

EAL's second possibility for you is its Senior Discount,

for which you must simply prove you are 62. This gives you and a travel mate of any age a 10 percent discount on any fare (along with frequent-flyer credits), with no restrictions on the days of travel. Remember, however, it always pays to check whether you're getting the lowest available fare when you get a discount.

And the third Eastern choice: Senior Discount Coupons, again for those 62 and up. These provide you with four one-way trips to anywhere the airline flies for $368 ($92 per trip) or eight one-way trips for $616 ($77 per trip). Seats are limited and cannot be reserved before six days prior to departure. You may travel only from noon Monday through noon Thursday and all day Saturday. Frequent-flyer credits? Yes.

For information: Call your travel agent or 1-800-EASTERN (1-800-327-8376).

NORTHWEST

Northwest's World Perks Senior Program is designed for travelers who are 62 or more, giving a 10 percent discount off all published fares to you and the person who's traveling with you (who may be any age), even when you're flying to Canada, Mexico, Jamaica, Europe, or Asia. All flights earn you frequent-flyer mileage, tour packages, and a quarterly newsletter. Although you must sign up and become a member to get the discount, there is no membership fee.

Members are eligible to purchase Northwest's Ultra-fare Coupon Books, with each coupon good for a one-way flight in the continental United States and Canada (flights to Hawaii or Alaska cost two coupons each). Again, you must fly on Tuesdays, Wednesdays, Thursdays, or Saturdays, make your reservations at least 14 days in advance, and remember that there are some

holiday blackouts. Four-coupon books currently cost $384 ($96 per trip), eight-coupon books $640 ($80 per trip). Flights earn you frequent-flyer credits.
For information: Call your travel agent or 1-800-225-2525 for reservations. Call 1-800-678-2700 to enroll in the World Perks Senior Program.

PAN AMERICAN WORLD AIRWAYS
Pan American takes 10 percent off any published fare (except special senior discounted fares) within the U.S. and to most destinations in Europe for those who have reached their 62nd birthdays and a younger traveling companion.

Pan Am also offers a good deal on its shuttle flights to or from New York and Washington, DC, or Boston if you are 65. Your current one-way fare is only $49, while the regular fares as this book goes to press is $119 during the week and $79 on weekends. You may fly only at these hours, however: 10:30 A.M. to 2:30 P.M. and 7:30 P.M. to 9:30 P.M., Monday through Friday; all day Saturday; and until 2:30 P.M. on Sunday. You are guaranteed a seat. Simply show up, with proof of age, half an hour before flight time. Frequent-flyer credits apply.
For information: Call your travel agent or 1-800-221-1111.

TWA
This airline reduces the fare by 10 percent for travelers over 62 and a companion of any age on almost all flights in the U.S. and Puerto Rico and some to Europe as well (England and Italy, for example). Ask for the discount when you make your reservations. You'll get frequent-flyer credits for your mileage.

The Senior Travel Pak is the second alternative offered

by TWA. Currently priced at $379, this gives you four coupons good for up to 2,000 miles one way per coupon within the United States, Puerto Rico, and Nassau, plus a bonus coupon that allows you to purchase a round-trip ticket to Europe at a good discount. You must fly on Tuesday, Wednesday, Thursday, or Saturday within the lower 48 states or to the Caribbean Islands. Travel to Hawaii costs two coupons each way from any mainland point if the trip is more than 2,000 miles or is made during a peak travel season.

Your third option is the TWA Takeoff Pass, on which you're entitled to a 10 percent discount if you are 62. At this moment the pass costs $1,995 for everyone else, but you get it for $1,795.50. This entitles you to a year of travel that includes one round-trip to Europe, one round-trip to Hawaii, one round-trip to the Bahamas or Puerto Rico, and three round-trips in the continental U.S. You may choose an 18-month pass for $150 more if you think you won't be able to fit that much travel into a year. No frequent-flyer credits or upgrades are given for these flights. More details: flights to Europe must be booked 21 to 45 days in advance; and you may not fly on Friday, Saturday, or Sunday; flights to the other destinations must be reserved 7 to 45 days in advance, and you may not fly on Friday or Sunday to points within the U.S. or Hawaii.

For information: Call your travel agent or 1-800-221-2000 for reservations. Call 1-800-872-8374 for the Takeoff Pass.

UNITED AIRLINES

Here you'll get 10 percent off coach/economy round-trip excursion fares if you're 62 or more, and so will a companion of any age. You are entitled to frequent-flyer credits on these flights.

Another opportunity: United's senior travel club, called Silver Wings Plus, is open to you if you are over 60 (although you don't get discounted fares until you are 62). For $50 you can become a lifetime member but get your money back in the form of a $50 discount certificate for travel within a year. For an additional $100 you may buy a companion membership with two discount certificates worth $50 each. This means your travel mate (who may change from trip to trip and who may be any age) receives the same privileges you do when you travel together. With your membership you'll get discounts on hotels, rental cars, and travel packages. You'll be automatically enrolled in the frequent-flyer program, get credits for miles, and receive a quarterly magazine.

On your 62nd birthday Silver Wings Plus starts giving you a 10 percent discount on all applicable published fares to destinations in the U.S., Canada, Mexico, Singapore, Australia, New Zealand, Taiwan, China, Korea, Thailand, the Philippines, and even a few major cities in Europe. Your membership also gives you a discount of 10 percent on United Express, British Airways, Alitalia, KLM, and Iberia flights to Europe.

There's still a third variety of opportunity offered to mature travelers by United: United's Flight Pack gives you a book of four coupons for $420 ($105 per trip) or eight coupons for $704 ($88 per trip), with each coupon good for up to 2,000 miles one way anywhere in the U.S. You may fly any day of the week, although there are some blackout periods at peak times. Seats are limited, and you must make your reservations and exchange your coupon for a ticket at least 14 days prior to travel. Yes, you'll earn frequent-flyer points for your mileage.

For information: Call your travel agent or 1-800-241-6522. Call 1-800-628-2868 for United Silver Wings Plus.

USAir

One variety of senior savings on USAir (which has acquired Piedmont) is its straight 10 percent discount (with frequent-flyer mileage credits) for travelers 62 and older. When you fly with a companion, that person also gets the discount.

Another choice is USAir's Senior Discount Coupon Books: $420 ($105 per trip) for four one-way coupons or $704 ($88 per trip) for eight one-way coupons that may be traded for tickets to any destination within the continental United States, including flights on affiliated commuter lines. The coupon books may be purchased when you are 62. You must use them up within a year of purchase and book your trips at least 14 days before you travel. There are some blackout periods around holidays, but you'll accumulate mileage points in the frequent-flyer program.

For information: Call your travel agent or 1-800-428-4322.

VIRGIN ATLANTIC AIRLINES

Virgin Atlantic cuts fares to London from JFK, Newark, Los Angeles, or Miami for the over-60 population during off-peak periods, with the rate dependent on the date of departure. You must book your flight at least 30 days before the flight and be prepared to verify your age. Cancellations must be made 21 days before departure. Check this deal out, but compare the fares to the airline's off-peak specials that are offered to everyone. These bargain rates, usually better than the over-60 discount, require that you pay when you make your reservations and are nonrefundable. Virgin Atlantic has no mileage program.

For information: Call your travel agent or 1-800-862-8621.

U.S. REGIONAL AIRLINES

ALASKA AIRLINES

Alaska Airlines gives you, at 62, and a traveling companion a 10 percent discount on most flights in and out of the state. Sometimes, during the off-seasons, the special senior fares are even better. Inquire about them before making a decision.

For information: Call your travel agent or 1-800-426-0333.

ALOHA AIRLINES

Aloha, which flies only among the Hawaiian Islands, charges those over 65 a fare of $39.95 one way. That's $10 cheaper than the full fare for everyone else.

For information: Call your travel agent or 1-800-367-5250.

AMERICA WEST

This airline has two offers for you at 62. The first is its Senior Saver Pack, a coupon book good for a year that currently gives you four one-way flights wherever it flies within the continental U.S. for $348, or eight one-way trips for $598. Two coupons are required per trip for flights to Honolulu or to East Coast cities. Travel days are limited to noon on Monday through noon on Thursday and all day Saturday. Seats are limited, and reservations must be made 14 days in advance. There are some blackout periods.

In addition, America West offers its Senior Fare that gives you a discount of 10 percent on normal coach fares. Ask whether it is the lowest fare available to you on the days you want to fly.

For information: Call your travel agent or 1-800-247-5692.

HAWAIIAN AIR

Here, too, you may fly inter-island for $39.95 per segment if you are 65, less than the regular full fare. At 62, you can get a 10 percent discount off any published fare on flights to and from the mainland U.S., and so can your traveling companion.

For information: Call your travel agent or 1-800-367-5320.

MIDWAY AIRLINES

Based in Chicago, Midway is another airline that takes 10 percent off any published fare for you at 62 and a traveling companion of any age.

For information: Call your travel agent or 1-800-621-5700.

MIDWEST EXPRESS

Ten percent is taken off the fare for people over 65 on all fares to all destinations. The discount also applies to Skyway Airlines.

For information: Call your travel agent or 1-800-452-2022.

SOUTHWEST AIRLINES

Flying mainly in the southwestern United States, this company offers special low fares to travelers over 65 on

all flights. We are told that the senior fares (e.g., $19 from Phoenix to Los Angeles at this writing as opposed to the regular unrestricted fare of $39) are the lowest the airline sells. If you fly 20 one-way trips with Southwest, by the way, you'll get a free round-trip anywhere it flies.
For information: Call your travel agent or 1-800-531-5601

GOOD DEALS ON CANADIAN AIRLINES

AIR CANADA
If you're over 62, you are eligible for substantial discounts that vary according to the route—and frequent-flyer credits. But check out the special promotional fares to see if the senior discount is more or less advantageous.

Air Canada's seasonal Freedom Flyer program is another possibility to look into. Available at certain times of the year, it allows passengers 55 or over, and a companion of any age, to visit up to 12 cities in the United States and Canada at reduced fares on Air Canada or its connector airlines. All destinations on a single ticket must be visited on the same trip. You may stop over only once in any city, the nonrefundable tickets must be purchased at least 14 days in advance, and you may change flights but not destinations for a change fee of $75 (Canadian dollars). With these fares you will earn frequent-flyer credits.
For information: Call your travel agent or 1-800-776-3000.

CANADIAN AIRLINES INTERNATIONAL
Here you'll get a special discount on most fares on domestic flights within Canada if you are over 62. This

beats most other supersaver fares, although a "seat sale" may produce a lower price. Book 14 days in advance and have proof of age. No restrictions on time, day, or season. **For information:** Call your travel agent or 1-800-426-7000.

GOOD DEALS ON FOREIGN AIRLINES

Again, always inquire about special senior discounts when you book a flight, even if you don't see them listed here. Airlines change their policies with very little notice. Your travel agent can provide current information.

AIR FRANCE
Special senior citizen fares are available to you if you are over 65 (or sometimes over 60) on flights in France and occasionally on other flights within Europe. No savings because of age, however, when you fly to or from the U.S. **For information:** Call your travel agent or 1-800-237-2747.

ALITALIA
If you are a member of United Silver Wings Plus travel club and are over 65, you are eligible for a 10 percent discount on Alitalia flights. **For information:** Call your travel agent or 1-800-223-5730.

BRITISH AIRWAYS
British Airways' major bonus for its "mature clientele" (people over the age of 60 and their companions over 50) is the Privileged Traveller program, which you must join for a fee of $10 for two years (no fee the next time

around). You will receive a card that serves as your proof of age and contains a record of your meal and seat preferences, as well as any special medical needs.

The card entitles you to special senior economy-class fares with 10 percent savings on all other fares between the U.S. and the UK, including club, first class, and *Concorde*. There are no penalties for cancellations or changed itineraries before departure from the U.S., nor are there blackout periods. The same 10 percent comes off all British Airways Holiday Tours and travel on the Venice-Simplon *Orient Express*. You're entitled to the same 10 percent discount from British Airways if you belong to United Airlines Silver Wings Plus Club.

Added feature: as a Privileged Traveller, you may preboard the plane.

For information: Call your travel agent or 1-800-AIR-WAYS (1-800-247-9297).

EL AL
Anyone over the age of 60 is entitled to El Al's Golden Age Fare, which gives you a discount of about 15 percent off the regular Apex fare to Israel. You may stay for up to two months and may make one stopover in Europe. A 14-day advance purchase is required, and there is a $50 fee for changing your return flight.

But, before accepting this deal, check out whether the cheaper Superapex fare (with a maximum stay of 21 days) will work out better for you.

For information: Call your travel agent or 1-800-223-6700 (212-768-9200 in New York).

FINNAIR
This airline gives good discounts to those age 65 and

over on flights from New York or Los Angeles to Helsinki. The catch is that you cannot book your flight until three days before departure. However, the fares are available all year, and you may take a younger spouse along at the same price.

For information: Call your travel agent or 1-800-950-5000.

IBERIA

If you are a member of United Airlines' Silver Wings Plus travel club, you will get 10 percent off most published fares on Iberia.

For information: Call your travel agent or 1-800-772-4642.

KLM ROYAL DUTCH AIRLINES

KLM lowers the fares somewhat for travelers over 60 and their spouses on flights from the United States to several cities in the Netherlands—but only in the off-season. KLM also participates in the United Silver Wings Plus travel club, entitling members to the same 10 percent discount on all applicable published fares.

For information: Call your travel agent or 1-800-777-5553.

LUFTHANSA

At age 62, you can get a 10 percent reduction on most coach or Apex fares for yourself and a younger travel mate, on flights from gateway cities in the U.S. to Germany.

For information: Call your travel agent or 1-800-645-3880.

MEXICANA

A senior discount of 10 percent applies to all Mexicana fares between gateway cities in the U.S. and Mexico, including stopovers, except in July and August. You must be 62, but your traveling companion may be younger and get the same rate. There are blackouts around major holidays.

For information: Call your travel agent or 1-800-531-7921.

SABENA

Special senior fares, costing about the same as Apex but more flexible, are the offer from Sabena on flights to Tel Aviv or Warsaw. You must be 60 years old. At 62, you're also entitled to a 10 percent discount on some fares to European destinations.

For information: Call your travel agent or 1-800-632-8050.

SAS (SCANDANAVIAN AIRLINES)

If you are 65, this airline charges you a little less on some internal flights within Sweden.

For information: Call your travel agent or 1-800-221-2350.

SWISS AIR

What you'll get from Swiss Air are special senior fares at age 60 on flights from East Coast gateway cities to Warsaw, Poland. In addition, you are entitled to special fares within Europe on some flights, usually at 65 but sometimes at 60 or 62. Check out the possibilities when you buy your tickets.

For information: Call your travel agent or 1-800-221-4750.

TAP AIR PORTUGAL

The senior discount here, for those over 60, is minimal and is available only during the off-peak season, usually from September 15 until the end of May. You may fly any day of the week and get the same fare for a traveling companion.

For information: Call your travel agent or 1-800-221-7370.

Chapter Eight

Beating the Costs of Car Rentals

N ever rent a car without getting a discount or a special promotional rate. Almost all car-rental agencies in the United States and Canada give them to all manner of customers, including those who belong to over-50 organizations (see Chapter 19) and airline senior clubs (see Chapter 7). The discount that's coming to you as a member can save you a lot of money. Refer to the membership material sent by the group to which you belong for specific information about your discount privileges.

But, first, keep in mind:

▶ Don't grab your member discount too hastily because you may belong to some other organization that will save you even more. Or specials may be offered that week or month that prove to be even better deals. So, always ask for the *best rate available* at that moment— mentioning, of course, the groups to which you belong.
▶ When you call to ask about rates or reservations, always be armed with your organization's ID number and your own membership card for reference.
▶ The savings may not be available at all locations, so

you must check them out each time you make a reservation.

Here are the car-rental agencies that are currently offering you special rates or discounts.

ALAMO
This car-rental company's news is that it gives an Experienced Driver Discount at most of its locations to members of AARP, Days Inns' September Days Club, and Delta Air Lines' Young at Heart Coupon Program.
For information: Call 1-800-327-9633.

AVIS
Special rates, amounting to 5 to 10 percent off regular rates, are given to members of AARP, CARP (Canadian Association of Retired Persons), and Mature Outlook.
For information: Call 1-800-331-1800.

BUDGET/SEARS RENT-A-CAR
Participating Budget/Sears locations give discounts to members of Mature Outlook, AARP, and many other lesser-known 50-plus or senior groups. The usual saving is $5 per day on weekday rates and $2 per day on weekly and weekend rates.
For information: Call 1-800-527-0700.

DOLLAR
Discounts, which vary according to location, are offered to AARP members at 50 and anyone else over 60.
For information: Call 1-800-421-6868.

HERTZ

If you are a member of AARP, Mature Outlook, or Y.E.S., you will be entitled to savings, usually from 5 to 10 percent, on Hertz rental cars. In addition, Hertz gives discounts to members of United Airlines' Silver Wings Plus travel club, and Days Inns' September Days Club.
For information: Call 1-800-654-3131.

NATIONAL

With this rent-a-car agency, you can get special rates and discounts if you are a member of Mature Outlook or AARP.
For information: Call 1-800-328-4567.

THRIFTY RENT-A-CAR

AARP members get a 10 percent discount on rentals any day of the week. Members of CARP and Days Inns' September Days Club are also entitled to senior discounts.
For information: Call 1-800-367-2277.

Chapter Nine
Saving a Bundle on Trains and Buses in North America

Getting around town, especially if you live in a city where driving is not a practical option, probably means depending on public transportation to get you from hither to yon. Remember that, once you reach a particular birthday—in most cases, your 60th or 65th—you can take advantage of some good senior markdowns on trains, buses, and subways (unfortunately taxis have yet to join the movement). All you need is a senior ID card issued by your city or county to play this game, which usually reduces fares by half. Although you may find it uncomfortable at the beginning to pull out that card and flash it at the bus driver or ticket agent, it soon becomes automatic and you will realize some nice savings.

Seniors can find bargains on long-distance rail and bus travel as well.

RIDING THE RAILS

Probably every commuter railroad in the United States and Canada gives older riders a break, although you may have to do your traveling during off-peak periods when the trains are not filled with go-getters rushing to and from their offices. Ask for your discount when you purchase your ticket.

As for serious long-distance travel, many mature travelers are addicted to the railroads, finding riding the rails a leisurely, relaxed, romantic, comfortable, economical, and satisfying way to make miles while enjoying the scenery.

So many passes and discounts on railroads are available to travelers heading for other parts of the world that sorting them out becomes confusing. But, once you do, they will help stretch your dollars while covering a lot of ground.

See the country-by-country section in Chapter 4 for the best deals on trains in foreign countries for travelers of a certain age. Also check out the sight-seeing trips run by Omni Senior Rail Tours (page 51).

AMTRAK
To lure mature travelers, Amtrak now offers a discount of 25 percent on regular one-way fares to people over 65. You must buy your ticket before boarding the train and be ready to prove your age. Remember that there are blackout periods when this fare isn't available; these are usually during the major holidays or other peak travel seasons.

Now, some words of wisdom: Do not assume that the senior fare is the best bargain. Always mention the senior discount, but be sure you get the *lowest fare available*. On Amtrak's family fare, for example, one member of a couple traveling together pays full fare, the other half fare. (Children 12 through 21 pay half fare, and children 2 through 11 pay only 25 percent.) Thus the cost to couples is the same (25 percent off), but the blackout periods do not apply. You may travel at these family fare rates year-round, any day, any time.

For information: Call Amtrak at 1-800-USA-RAIL.

VIA RAIL CANADA

The government-owned Canadian passenger railroad offers those 60 and over a one-third reduction on the regular coach fare, one way or round-trip, every day of the year, with no restrictions—not even on Christmas Day. The discount does not apply to club seats or sleepers.

In the off-season, however, better deals are Via Rail's Seat Sales which anyone can get at any age. This gives a 40 percent discount on both the basic fare and club chairs or sleepers and then, for you if you're over 60, an additional 10 percent, bringing it to a 50 percent reduction. The catch is that this good deal is not available in the peak summer season, usually June through September.

For information: Call Via Rail Canada's toll-free numbers, which differ for each region of the country. Get the number for your area by dialing 1-800-555-1212.

LET THEM DO THE DRIVING: GOING BY BUS

Never, never board a bus without showing the driver your senior ID card, because even the smallest bus lines in the tiniest communities in this country and abroad give senior discounts, usually half fare. In Europe, your senior rail pass is often valid on major motorcoach lines as well, so always be sure to ask.

GREYHOUND LINES

If you decide to let Greyhound do the driving, you are entitled to a 10 percent reduction on any full fare, any day of the year, in the United States and Canada, if you are 65 and show proof of age when you purchase your tickets. But keep in mind that there may be "specials" or promotional fares that will save you even more money, so always ask for the cheapest fare available at the time you want to travel. You may even want to change your traveling dates so that you may take advantage of a lower fare. Your 10 percent over-65 discount cannot be added to the specials.

For information: Call your local Greyhound reservations office.

TRAILWAYS LINES

We're listing this bus line separately, even though it has recently merged with Greyhound, because some bus routes retain the name. The senior perk of a 10 percent discount for those over 65 applies even when the motorcoach is labeled Trailways Lines.

GRAY LINE TOURS

Gray Line is an association of many small independent motorcoach lines throughout the country, all of which offer sight-seeing and package tours. Most, but not all, of them give a 15 percent discount on half- and full-day sight-seeing tours to members of AARP at age 50 and sometimes other seniors as well. Find out if you qualify before buying your ticket.

For information: Call the Gray Line Tours office in your area.

VOYAGEUR

This Canadian motorcoach line's Club 60 offers you one-third off regular fares on its regular bus service throughout the provinces of Ontario and Quebec. No need to join anything; simply present proof that you are 60 when you buy your tickets. No restrictions on day or time. You'll also get a discount on Voyageur's one-day tours by bus or riverboat out of such major cities as Montreal, Ottawa, and Toronto.

A really good deal, one that may profit you even more than your one-third discount if you plan to do considerable wandering in these provinces, is the TourPass. Check it out before buying your tickets.

For information: Call the Voyageur office in your area.

ONTARIO NORTHLAND

An excursion railroad that takes you on wilderness tours of Canada's north country through areas accessible only by rail or plane, Ontario Northland offers mature travelers some fine price reductions. For example, the Polar Bear Express, an excursion from Cochrane, Ontario, to Moosonee near James Bay, operates from the end of June until Labor Day except on Fridays and sells senior tickets for 50 percent off the regular fare.

For information: Ontario Northland, 65 Front St. West, Toronto, ON M5J 1E6, Canada; 416-965-4268.

Chapter Ten

Hotels and Motels: Get Your Over-50 Markdowns

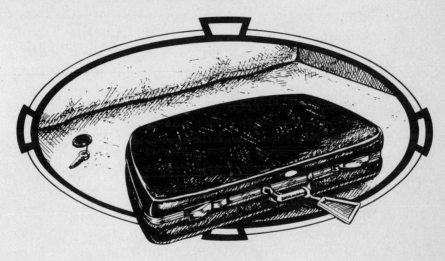

Across the United States and Canada, major chains of hotels and motels (and individual establishments as well) are chasing the mature market. (That's you.) As a candidate for an increasing barrage of bargains in lodgings, you may not have to sell all the family jewels to afford your next trip.

To get your discounts at most establishments, all that's required is evidence that you are 55, or 60, or 65, as the case may be. Or that you are a member of a club that makes many of the same savings available to you at 50. When you join the American Association of Retired Persons (you needn't be retired), Mature Outlook, or a similar organization, you will receive a list of the lodging chains that offer special rates to reward you for having lived so long.

But, first, keep in mind:

If you want to take advantage of the discounts coming to you, be sure to do some advance scouting and planning with your travel agent or on your own.

▶ In this rapidly changing world, rates and policies can be altered in a flash, so an update is always advisable.

▶ Information about discounts is seldom volunteered; in most cases, you must arrange for them when you make your reservations and remind the desk clerk of them again when you check in. Do not wait until you're settling your bill because then it may be too late.

▶ Usually, over-50 discounts are subject to "space availability." That means it may be pretty hard to get them when you want to travel. So always book early, demanding your discount privileges, and try to be flexible on your dates in order to take advantage of them. Your best bets for space are usually weekends in large cities, weekdays at resorts, and non–holiday seasons.

▶ It's quite possible that a special promotional rate, especially in off-peak seasons or on weekends, may save you more money than your senior discount. Many hotels, especially in big cities and warm climes, cut their prices drastically in the summer, for example. Others that cater mostly to business people during the week try to encourage weekend traffic by offering bargain rates if you stay over a Saturday night. Resorts are often eager to fill their rooms on weekdays. So always investigate all the possibilities before you get too enthusiastic about using your hard-earned discount, and remember to ask for the *lowest available rate*.

▶ There are several chains of no-frills budget motels that don't offer discounts or too much in the way of amenities but do charge very low room rates and tend to be located along the most-traveled routes.

▶ In most cases, not every hotel or inn in a chain will

offer the discount. Those that do are called "participating" hotels/motels.
▶ In addition to the chains, many individual hotels and inns are eager for your business and offer special reduced rates. Always *ask* before making a reservation. Your travel agent should be able to help you with this.
▶ Some hotel restaurants will give you a discount too, usually whether or not you are a registered guest.
▶ By the way, your discount will not be given on top of other special discounts. One discount is all you get.

ASTON HOTELS AND RESORTS
Aston's Sun Club gives you at age 62—and your traveling companions—a discount of about 20 percent on the room rates at its hotels in Hawaii, California, and Mexico. Sometimes it also throws in a free subcompact rental car, meal discounts, and gifts. Ask for the special rates and other offerings when you reserve your room and take proof of your age with you when you check in.
For information: Call 1-800-922-7866.

BEST WESTERN
This huge chain of independently owned motels offers a 10 percent discount on the room rates to people over 55 years of age at more than 1,300 of its properties in the United States and Canada. If you belong to AARP, you get the discount at 50. Advance reservations are required, and so is proof of age when you check in.
For information: Call 1-800-528-1234.

BUDGETEL INNS
Budgetel Inns are inexpensive motels located in 20 states, mostly in the South and Midwest. About half of

them will give you a 10 percent discount if you are 55 years old, so check this out when you make your reservations.
For information: Call 1-800-428-3438.

CALINDA QUALITY INNS

These hotels, part of the Quality Inns International chain, in 13 locations in Mexico take 30 percent off the room rates and, in most locations, 15 percent off food and beverages for members of AARP and other senior organizations. But you must make reservations at least 30 days in advance and pay a one-night deposit with a major credit card. And there are no refunds unless you cancel 30 days before check-in time. An alternative plan is the Prime Time program that gives AARP members at 50 and anyone over 60 an uncomplicated 10 percent discount.
For information: Call 1-800-228-5151.

CLARION HOTELS AND RESORTS

See Quality Inns.

COLONY HOTELS AND RESORTS

You will get a 25 percent discount here if you belong to AARP or 20 percent otherwise simply because you are over 59. These hotels are located on five Hawaiian islands and in nine mainland states.
For information: Call 1-800-367-6046.

COMFORT INNS

See Quality Inns.

COMPRI HOTELS

If you are 60—or 50 and a member of "a recognized senior organization"—you are entitled to approximately 15 percent off the room rates at these 24 hotels scattered around the United States and Canada. Breakfast, cocktails, and late-night snacks are included.
For information: Call 1-800-426-6774.

COUNTRY HEARTH INNS

A string of low-cost motels, Country Hearth Inns take 10 percent off the room rate if you can prove you're over 50 years of age.
For information: Call 1-800-848-5767 or, in Ohio, 1-800-282-5711.

COUNTRY INN COLLECTION

This is a group of charming and picturesque country inns sprinkled throughout New England, in areas such as northeastern Maine, the White Mountains of New Hampshire, the Green Mountains of Vermont, the Berkshires of Massachusetts, and the lake and valley regions of Connecticut. All of them offer a discount of 10 percent on room rates to visitors over 60. Most of the inns are in restored historic buildings and offer beautiful scenery, good food, warmth, and hospitality. You may arrange an inn-to-inn vacation or choose among these special places.
For information: Call 1-800-852-4667 (in Vermont and Canada, call 802-496-3221).

COURTYARD BY MARRIOTT

A mid-priced hotel chain run by the Marriott Corporation, Courtyard gives a 15 percent discount on room rates at most of its 150 locations around the country to

members of AARP and some discounts to other seniors. Just mention your membership when you reserve your room.
For information: Call 1-800-321-2211.

CROWNE PLAZA HOTELS
See Holiday Inns.

DAYS INNS, HOTELS, SUITES, AND DAY STOPS
One of the largest lodging chains in this country and abroad, Days Inns invites you at age 50 to join its September Days Club, entitling you to 15 percent to 40 percent off rooms at about 1,000 participating hotels, motels, suites, and lodges. You also get 10 percent off your meals at participating Days Inns restaurants and your purchases at its gift shops, discounts on rental cars, discounts on prescription and over-the-counter drugs, discounts on entertainment attractions and theme parks, trips and escorted tours at group rates, information on last-minute travel bargains, a quarterly travel magazine, and a lot more perks. Membership costs $12 a year for you and your spouse. Most inns also give AARP members 10 percent off on rooms.
For information: Call 1-800-241-5050.

DORAL HOTELS
You can get a one-bedroom suite at any of the four Doral hotels in New York City for $150 per night, or a deluxe room for $110, on a space available basis, if you are over the age of 60. Such accommodations normally range from $200 to $700 per night. A continental breakfast is included, as are free parking on Friday and Saturday nights (except at the Doral Inn) and a booklet listing

discounts at New York attractions. In addition, a concierge is on hand to help you make reservations and travel arrangements.

For information: Call 1-800-223-5823 outside of New York state. In New York, call 212-752-5700 or the individual hotels.

DOUBLETREE HOTELS

These luxury hotels, concentrated in the West, give Silver Leaf discounts of about 15 percent to older travelers, but each determines its own policy, so you'll have to check the specific hotel that interests you to find out what it offers.

For information: Call 1-800-528-0444.

DRURY INNS

These budget motels offer a 10 percent discount on the regular room rates at all of their 41 locations to AARP members at 50 and others who are 55-plus. Just ask and have your proof of age handy.

For information: Call 1-800-325-8300.

ECONO LODGES

With a string of 550 budget motels in 47 states and Canada, this chain provides a 10 percent discount at most of its properties to AARP members and anybody over 55. It also has a Frequent Travelers Plan: for every six nights you spend within one year at the same participating motel you get a seventh night free.

For information: Call 1-800-446-6900.

ECONOMY INNS OF AMERICA

This economy lodging chain, with motels located near major highways in California, Florida, South Carolina, and Georgia, gives 10 percent off the already low room

rates to AARP members and anyone over 55. Just ask for it.
For information: Call 1-800-826-0778.

EMBASSY SUITES HOTELS
These hotels feature two-room suites with free breakfast and complimentary cocktails and take up to 10 percent off the regular room rates for members of AARP, the National Retired Teachers Association, and the National Council of Senior Citizens. That is, if they are participating in the program. If you're not a cardholder, you'll get the discount anyway at most of the hotels just for being over 65—in some cases, only 55.
For information: Call 1-800-362-2779.

FAIRFIELD INNS BY MARRIOTT
You'll get a 15 percent discount at these economy motels whenever you mention your AARP membership, except during special events. Nonmembers get 10 percent discounts at 62.
For information: Call 1-800-228-2800.

FRIENDSHIP INNS
A chain of motels in about 100 cities, most Friendship Inns will give you a 10 percent discount if you are over 65 or belong to AARP. Be sure to ask for it when you check in.
For information: Call 1-800-453-4511.

GUEST QUARTERS
A small chain with about 30 locations and one-bedroom suites only, Guest Quarters takes off 10 percent for members of AARP at most of its hotels.
For information: Call 1-800-424-2900.

HAMPTON INNS

The LifeStyle 50 program offers a four-for-one deal for people over 50. This means a guest may share a double room with three other adults over 50 at any of the 216 Hampton Inns around the country and pay only the *single* rate. Free continental breakfasts come with the room. Simply show proof that you are over 50 when you check in and sign up for a free LifeStyle 50 membership card there and then. Or you may get an application by calling the number below.

For information: Call 1-800-HAMPTON.

HARLEY HOTELS

Look for a 10 percent discount at all of these hotels—except those in New York City—simply by flashing your AARP or other senior organization card.

For information: Call 1-800-321-2323.

HILTON HOTELS

Hilton's Senior HHonors travel club is an excellent deal for you if you're 60 years old. As a member you are entitled to 25 to 50 percent off the room rates at 240 Hilton Hotels in the United States and 70 Hilton International Hotels in 32 countries. You also get 20 percent off the bill on dinner for two at the hotel restaurants in the United States, whether or not you are a hotel guest. The Senior HHonors room rates are also available to your children, parents, or grandchildren and are guaranteed to be the lowest published rates offered. Membership costs $25 a year in the United States or $50 a year worldwide ($150 for life worldwide) and includes your spouse.

For information: Call 1-800-445-8667.

HOLIDAY INNS

Your best bet here is to join Sears' Mature Outlook, because members of this over-50 club get room rates reduced by 20 percent at participating Holiday Inns and Holiday Inn Crowne Plaza Hotels worldwide. Not only that, but members also have 10 percent deducted from their food bills at any of the hotel restaurants whether they are staying at the inn or just dropping by for a meal. Ask for a Mature Outlook application at the reservations desk or call 1-800-336-6330 to have one sent to you. If you belong to a senior group other than Mature Outlook, you are entitled to a 10 percent discount on room rates. Ask for it when you make your reservations and again at check-in.

For information: Call 1-800-HOLIDAY.

HOWARD JOHNSON

Howard Johnson Road Rally, a special program for people over 59 and for over-50 card-carrying members of recognized senior organizations, offers up to 30 percent off regular room rates. Just check into a participating HJ and show your ID. But it's best to book ahead because, at some times of the year, the number of rooms available at 30 percent off is limited. In any case, you will always get at least a 15 percent reduction.

For information: Call 1-800-634-3464.

HYATT HOTELS

These are all individually owned, and therefore each hotel offers its own discounts. Those in big cities or major resort areas rarely have senior rates, but others may take 10 to 50 percent off the room rate. Hotels in resort areas tend to make their most generous offers in the off-season.

For information: Call 1-800-228-9000.

INN SUITES

With nine inns in Arizona and California this small chain will give you—at age 55—a 10 percent discount on regular room rates on its one- and two-room suites. Included is complimentary breakfast, a morning newspaper, and a free cocktail hour.

For information: Call 1-800-842-4242.

KNIGHTS INNS/ARBORGATE INNS

This budget motel chain with about 200 locations mostly in the Southeast gives a discount of 10 percent throughout the year to anyone over 55.

For information: Call 1-800-722-7220.

LA QUINTA MOTOR INNS

With about 200 locations mostly in the Sunbelt, these motor inns are inexpensive and become even more so when you ask for your 10 percent discount. You'll get it if you are a member of AARP, Mature Outlook, or a similar organization or if you are 55 and can prove it. It is sometimes not available during special events in a particular location. La Quinta also offers its Senior Class program for people over 60. For a one-time $10 membership fee, you are entitled to 20 percent off plus some other incidental benefits. Apply at any hotel in the chain

or write Senior Class, Box 27128, Minneapolis, MN
55427.
For information: Call 1-800-531-5900.

LK MOTELS
A budget chain in middle America, LK takes 10 percent
off for AARP members and anybody over 55.
For information: Call 1-800-848-5711.

MARRIOTT HOTELS & RESORTS
Marriott's Leisurelife Program may be one of the best
deals around—if you are 50 and belong to AARP or 62
otherwise. It gives you rooms at a 50 percent discount on
regular weekday rates for single, double, or family accommodations seven days a week at most of its hotels in
the United States, Canada, and many cities abroad, subject to availability. You may reserve up to two rooms at
half price so family members or friends traveling with
you can share your good fortune.

There's also a 25 percent discount on dining (except on
specials and alcoholic beverages) for your entire party of
up to eight people. This may be used as often as you like.
And there's a 10 percent discount on gift shop purchases
at any of Marriott's hotels and resorts. There are no
membership fees or cards, and guests must simply request the discount and present proof of age. What's
more, you need not be a hotel guest to get the restaurant
discount.

Advance room reservations are required. One hitch:
the room discounts may not be available at all times,
especially in peak seasons when there is high demand.
For information: Call 1-800-228-9290.

MASTER HOSTS INNS
See Red Carpet Inns.

NENDELS MOTOR INNS
A Pacific Northwest chain of 44 inns, Nendels takes 10 percent off the regular room rates for members of all senior organizations and those over 65. The discount is also available at Value Inns by Nendels. Request the discount when you make your reservation or check in.
For information: Call 1-800-547-0106.

OMNI HOTELS
Omni Hotels are another winner in this series. The participating hotels in this group—40 of them in the United States and Mexico—offer AARP members a 50 percent discount on regular room rates, based on space availability. You'll also get 15 percent off food and nonalcoholic beverages in their restaurants at all times if you are a registered hotel guest, and before 7 P.M. if you're not. To receive the special room rate, reserve ahead, request the discount, and be ready to provide your AARP card number. At check-in you will be asked to show your membership card. In the restaurants, present it before you place your order.
For information: Call 1-800-THE-OMNI.

OUTRIGGER HOTELS HAWAII
This chain with hotels all over the islands has come up with a Fifty Plus package that offers special rates—20 percent off the regular room rate—at its Honolulu locations.
For information: Call 1-800-733-7777.

PARK SUITES
Apply for a Senior Pass Card if you are 55 years of age or older and you'll save 25 percent off normal weekday rates and 10 percent off normal weekend rates for these two-room suites. With the card, you will also save 10 percent on the bill for food and beverages for a party of up to four in the hotel restaurants, even if you are not a registered guest. Grandchildren under 18 stay free in the same suite.
For information: Call 1-800-432-7272.

QUALITY INNS
Quality Inns International—which includes Quality Inns, Comfort Inns, Clarion Hotels and Resorts, Calinda Quality Inns, and Sleep Inns—operates more than 1,600 hotels worldwide. Most of them offer their Prime Time program, which gives 10 percent off the room rates any day of the year to guests who are 60 years old or members of AARP, United Silver Wings Plus, or another senior organization. The discount applies to the company's all-suite hotels as well as hotels and motels.

Even better, you can get a 30 percent reduction in rates at participating inns if you plan ahead. This Senior Saver rate is yours when you make your reservation at least 30 days in advance and pay a one-night deposit with a major credit card.
For information: Call 1-800-221-2222.

RADISSON HOTELS
Radisson will give you and family members traveling with you a discount of 10 to 25 percent on regular rates at all of its locations worldwide, based on availability. To get the lower rate you must have reached your 62nd

birthday and make advance reservations. Mention the discount when you reserve the room and again when you check in.

For information: Call 1-800-333-3333.

RAMADA INNS AND HOTELS

Ramada's Best Years Program is an excellent deal for you if you belong to any of a long list of senior organizations, including the over-50 clubs, or are 60 years old. It entitles you to 25 percent off the regular room rates at most of its 850 establishments in the U.S., as well as other parts of the world. Grandchildren up to 18 years of age may stay free if they share your room. There may be blackout periods, so reserve ahead.

For information: Call 1-800-272-6232.

RED CARPET INNS

Red Carpet Inns, Master Hosts Inns, and Scottish Inns are all operated by Hospitality International, and almost all of them in the United States and Canada give AARP members or anybody else who's 55 a 10 percent discount on room rates year-round, except perhaps during special local events such as spring break in Daytona Beach.

For information: Call 1-800-251-1962.

RED LION INNS/THUNDERBIRD INNS

To over-50s who present AARP or Mature Outlook cards, Red Lions and Thunderbirds—all in the western states—give their Prime Rate, which amounts to 20 percent off the regular room rates. Book ahead, because there are occasional blackout periods. In addition, their restaurants give you 10 percent off food chosen from the regular menu, except on holidays.

For information: Call 1-800-547-8010.

RED ROOF INNS

Red Roof Inns, the largest privately owned and operated economy lodging chain in the country, with over 200 locations in 30 states, offers a program called RediCard +60. For a $10 fee you may join the program at age 60, entitling you to a 10 percent discount on room rates, plus five coupons worth $2 each that are valid at any Red Roof Inn, rental car discounts, a road map in its own travel pouch, and a quarterly newsletter.
For information: Call 1-800-843-7663.

REGAL 8 INNS

If you are over 50, you will receive 10 percent off your bill at Regal 8 Inns, most of them located in the Midwest and Southwest. Simply present proof of age.
For information: Call 1-800-851-8888.

RESIDENCE INNS BY MARRIOTT

Participating inns in this chain of all-suite accommodations designed for extended stays offer a 15 percent discount on the rates to members of AARP.
For information: Call 1-800-331-3131.

RODEWAY INNS

With about 175 locations in the United States, Canada, and Mexico, Rodeway Inns ask only that you be 55 years old or a member of an over-50 club to get their 10 percent (or more) senior discount. Request the discount when you make your reservation.
For information: Call 1-800-228-2000.

SANDMAN HOTELS AND INNS

All situated in western Canada, these 20 inns take about

25 percent off the regular room rate if you are 55 or over. Write in advance for a Club 55 Card: 1755 W. Broadway, Ste. 310, Vancouver, BC V6J 4S5, Canada. **For information:** Call 1-800-663-6900.

SCOTTISH INNS
See Red Carpet Inns.

SHERATON HOTELS
Sheraton's hundreds of establishments all over the world give AARP members at 50 or anybody else at 65 a good break: a 25 percent discount on all but the minimum room rates. You'll need advance reservations and proper identification. The discount may not be available at peak periods.
For information: Call 1-800-325-3535.

SHONEY'S INNS
These 55 inexpensive motels are concentrated in the South. Because each is a franchise, policies vary, but most take 10 percent off the room rate for members of AARP and other "senior citizens."
For information: Call 1-800-222-2222.

SLEEP INNS
See Quality Inns.

SONESTA INTERNATIONAL HOTELS
This collection of 14 luxury hotels gives members of AARP a 10 percent discount at three of its establishments and a 15 percent discount at six others, including those in Amsterdam, New Orleans, and Bermuda. Re-

quest your special rate when you make your reservations.
For information: Call 1-800-343-7170.

STOUFFER HOTELS

Stouffer's Golden Years program gives guests over 60 a
room for about half the regular rate, single or double
occupancy. In one hotel, for example, the regular room
rate is $165 at this writing, while the Golden Years rate
is $80, so this is an opportunity worth considering. Ad-
vance reservations are required, rooms are limited to
availability, and the special rate does not apply to the
five Stouffer resorts. It's good any day of the week, year-
round. Some Stouffer Hotels also honor the AARP card
with a discount.
For information: Call 1-800-HOTELS-1.

SUPER 8 MOTELS

Many of the over 600 no-frills budget motels in this chain
give a discount to members of over-50 clubs or people
"over a certain age," that age differing according to the
location.
For information: Call 1-800-843-1991.

THUNDERBIRD MOTOR INNS

See Red Lion Inns.

TRAVELODGE

Travelodge offers a 15 percent discount on room rates to
members of just about any senior organization. Mention
your membership when you make reservations and/or
check in.
For information: Call 1-800-255-3050.

TREADWAY INNS

A small group of hotels in the East, Treadway Inns have discounts for those over 55 or members of such organizations as AARP and Mature Outlook. The savings vary from hotel to hotel but amount to about 10 to 15 percent. Ask for yours when you make reservations.
For information: Call 1-800-631-0182.

VAGABOND INNS

Concentrated on the West Coast, this chain of 43 inns has its Club 55 for mature travelers who are at least—three guesses—55! The club offers a special rate that gives you 10 to 20 percent off the regular single room rate. Not only that, but one to four adults may stay in your double room (with two double beds) at no extra charge at most of the hotels. Club membership costs nothing and gets you $10 in coupons good toward a stay at any Vagabond Inn and a quarterly newsletter outlining special senior travel events in the area. Join up at a Vagabond Inn, on the telephone (toll-free number below), or by writing to the club for an application. Another perk here is the Tenth Night program, which gives you a free night after you have racked up nine nights at any Vagabond Inns within a two-year period.
For information: Call 1-800-522-1555 or write to The Vagabond Inns Club 55, Box 85011, San Diego, CA 92138.

VISCOUNT HOTELS

At Viscount Hotels, affiliated with Travelodge, you are entitled to a 15 percent discount if you are a member of just about any senior organization, usual and unusual.

Ask for your discount when you make reservations or check in.

For information: Call 1-800-255-3050.

WESTIN HOTELS AND RESORTS

These luxury hotels often offer senior rates (often up to 50 percent off regular prices), but each has its own policy, so always ask about the possibilities when you make your reservations. Where there is no senior discount, ask for the weekend rate, usually 50 percent off, or the corporate rate, 20 to 25 percent off. All of these special rates, of course, are based on availability. If you belong to United Airlines Silver Wings Plus and rooms are available, you'll get a 50 percent reduction.

For information: Call 1-800-228-3000.

WESTMARK HOTELS

At all of the member hotels in Alaska and the Yukon you will get a 10 percent "senior citizen" discount, but only in the off-season, when it's a bit chilly up there—from October 1 through April 30.

For information: Call 1-800-544-0970.

GOOD DEALS IN RESTAURANTS

Many restaurants offer discounts to people in their prime, but in most cases you'll have to seek them out yourself, by asking or watching the ads in your local newspaper. In addition, a few large hotel chains will give you a break on your food bills when you eat in their restaurants. For example:

At **Hilton Hotels** restaurants in the U.S., you're entitled to a 20 percent discount on dinners for two, hotel guests or not, if you are a member of Hilton's Senior HHonors travel club.

Holiday Inn restaurants give a discount of 10 percent on the food check to members of Mature Outlook (see Chapter 19).

The restaurants in the **Marriott Hotels** will take 25 percent off your bill for a party of up to eight people if you are 62 or belong to AARP, whether or not you are staying at the hotel.

At **Omni Hotels** you'll get 15 percent taken off the check for food and nonalcoholic beverages in the hotel restaurants by flashing your AARP card. The discount is yours at any hour if you are staying at the hotel, but only before 7 P.M. if you are not.

If you have a Senior Pass card (free for over-55s), you will save 10 percent for a party of up to four at **Park Suites** restaurants.

The restaurants at **Red Lion Inns** and **Thunderbird Motor Inns** will reduce your food bill by 15 percent on regular-priced items if you belong to AARP or Mature Outlook. Be ready to produce your membership card.

Chapter Eleven

Alternative Lodgings for Thrifty Wanderers

I f you're willing to be innovative, imaginative, and occasionally fairly spartan, you can travel for a song or thereabouts. Here are some novel lodgings that can save you money and, at the same time, supply you with adventures worth talking about for years. They are not all designed specifically for people over 50, but each reports that a good portion of its clientele consists of free spirits of a certain age who are looking to beat the high cost of travel, meet people from other places, and have a real good time.

For more ways to cut travel costs and get smart in the bargain, check out the residential/educational programs in Chapter 16.

BIG APPLE ON A BUDGET

For visitors to New York City who do not wish to run up big hotel bills, inexpensive dormitory rooms are available in Hoboken, New Jersey, just across the river at Stephens Institute of Technology, 10 minutes by 24-hour bus to the big city. The rooms are even less expensive for people over 50 who mention this book. Rooms are limited during the school year, but many are available in the summer.

For information: Campus Holidays USA, 242 Bellevue Ave., Upper Montclair, NJ 07043; 1-800-526-2915.

CAMPUS TRAVEL SERVICE

More than 650 colleges and universities in the United States, Canada, and Europe open their dormitories to travelers every summer and during other school vacations. They offer spartan but adequate student rooms at bargain prices—an average of $18 a night—plus, in most cases, use of all campus facilities from swimming pool to cafeteria. Some include breakfast or, for not much more, three meals a day. Check with the colleges in the area you want to visit or get a copy of *U.S. and Worldwide Accommodations Guide* for $11.95 plus postage. This lists the campuses offering guest lodgings, the cost, the available dates, meal plans, and information about facilities and activities. The rooms—and occasionally bedroom suites—are usually available by the day, the week, or the month.

For information and the directory: Campus Travel Service, PO Box 5007, Laguna Beach, CA 92652; 714-497-3044.

THE EVERGREEN CLUB

This is a bed-and-breakfast club for singles or couples over 50 who have guest rooms in their homes that they're willing to make available to fellow club members traveling through their areas. No matter how elegant or simple your home is, no matter how close or far from the beaten path, the visitors pay $10 per night for single accommodations and $15 for double. You may not get rich on this scheme, but you will meet a lot of interesting people. And, in return, you may stay in other people's homes at the same prices when you're on the road.

Organized just a few years ago, the Evergreen Club now includes inexpensive, comfortable accommodations in about 400 homes in the United States, Canada, Mexico, Australia, Italy, France, New Zealand, Scotland, and Israel.

You pay $50 (per couple) or $40 (single) yearly dues. You'll get a membership card, an annual directory, and quarterly newsletters. The directory gives names and addresses of members, occupations and interests, policies about pets and smoking, and listings of nearby special attractions. Members make their own reservations and arrangements.

For information: Send a self-addressed, stamped envelope to the Evergreen Club, 1926 S. Pacific Coast Hwy., Ste. 217, Redondo Beach, CA 90277; 213-540-9600.

INNter LODGING CO-OP

Yet another way of sharing your home with other travelers and parlaying that guest room into virtually free lodging for yourself when you travel in the United States, Canada, and Europe. Guests pay about $5 per adult per night, depending upon whether there are private bathroom facilities. Children, who must arrive with their own sleeping bags, are an extra 25¢ a night. You must make your own arrangements directly with the hosts or the travelers who wish to stay with you.

When you join, you receive a membership card and a directory of participating hosts. Anyone any age may join, but the plan tends to appeal most to young families and mature travelers.

For information: INNter Lodging Co-op Services, PO Box 7044, Tacoma, WA 98407-0044; 206-756-0343.

NEW PALTZ SUMMER LIVING
If Florida is too hot for you in the summertime, consider spending a couple of months in the mountains, about 75 miles north of New York City. Every summer, while the usual student occupants are on vacation, 204 furnished garden apartments are reserved for seniors in the village of New Paltz, home of the State University of New York at New Paltz. The rents at this writing for the entire summer (from early June until late August) range from $1,900 to $3,200, depending on the size of the apartment. Living right in town next to the campus, you may audit college courses free and attend lectures and cultural events. There are two heated pools and a tennis court in the complex, as well as a clubhouse. Buses travel to New York every Wednesday for those who want to go to the theater, and there are frequent day trips to other places of interest.
For information: New Paltz Summer Living, 228 E. 45 St., Suite 1801, New York, NY 10017; 212-986-9193.

OAKWOOD RESORT APARTMENTS
Travelers over 55 may rent apartments in several states at a substantial discount during the winter months, choosing among locations in California, Texas, northern Virginia, Washington, DC, Atlanta, Las Vegas, Denver, and Raleigh, NC. You must rent for 30 days or longer from November 1 through the end of March to get the discount. All of the Oakwood Resort Apartments have kitchens and come completely furnished and equipped with TV, dishes, pots and pans, and linens. Weekly maid service and utilities are included. Most locations also

have swimming pools, tennis courts, party rooms, and fitness centers.

For information: Oakwood Resort Apartments, R&B Enterprises, 2222 Corinth Ave., Los Angeles, CA 90064; 1-800-421-6654.

SENIOR VACATION HOTELS OF FLORIDA

These hotels take a novel approach, with one-month minimum vacation packages year-round at four different hotels for seniors only (in Bradenton, Lakeland, and St. Petersburg). These are all-inclusive, with two meals, transportation, excursions, boat trips, entertainment, parties, and activities in the bundle. Current rates start at $850 (single) and $700 (per person, double) for a month in November, December, and April; more in January, February, or March. While the hotels will certainly accept you at age 50, you'll fit into the group more snugly if you're a bit more than that.

For information: Senior Vacation Hotels of Florida, 7401 Central Ave., St. Petersburg, FL 33710; 1-800-247-2203 (in Canada, 1-800-843-3713).

SENIORS ABROAD

Seniors Abroad is an international home-stay program exclusively for travelers over 50, offering an opportunity to stay in homes in other countries and learn firsthand how other people live. You pay your own costs which are reasonable because you have no hotel bills and many of your meals are home-cooked. Going overseas in escorted groups of 20 to 30 singles and couples, you spend three weeks in the country of your choice—Japan, Australia, New Zealand, Denmark, Sweden, or Norway—bunking for a few days or a week in different parts of the country with two or three different hosts who are also over 50.

Orientation, sight-seeing, and visits to U.S. embassies are included. If you wish to return the favor and host foreign visitors in your home, the same nonprofit organization will arrange that.

For information: Contact Evelyn Zivetz, Seniors Abroad, 12533 Pacato Circle North, San Diego, CA 92128; 619-485-1696.

SERVAS

Servas is "an international cooperative system of hosts and travelers established to help build world peace, goodwill, and understanding . . . among people of diverse cultures and backgrounds." A nonprofit, nongovernmental, interracial, and interfaith organization open to all ages, it provides lists of hosts, along with their activities and interests, all over the United States as well as the rest of the world. You make your own arrangements to stay with them, usually for two days, and share their everyday lives and concerns. No money changes hands. The hospitable people who take you in do this so they may enjoy your company and learn about you and your culture. You do the same for other travelers in return. There is a membership fee of $45 per year and you will be asked for two letters of reference and an interview.

For information: Send a #10 self-addressed, stamped envelope to US Servas, 11 John St., New York, NY 10038; 212-267-0252.

SUN CITY CENTER

Between Tampa and Sarasota in Florida, Sun City Center wants you to discover what a large self-contained retirement town is all about and offers a vacation package as a sample of life there. You may vacation here for four days (three nights), seven days, or three days. At this writing a stay of four days, three nights, per couple, with daily continental breakfast, two rounds of golf each, tennis, swimming, and club facilities, costs $90 from April 15 to September 30; $190 from October 1 to January 15; and $229 from February 1 to April 14.

For information: Sunmark Communities, PO Box 5698, Sun City Center, FL 33570; 1-800-237-8200 (in Florida, 1-800-282-8040).

SUN CITY WEST, SUN CITY TUCSON, AND SUN CITY LAS VEGAS

All three of these related retirement communities offer inexpensive vacation stays designed to give you a taste of what goes on in such a place and, of course, to persuade you to pack up and move in. One of you must be 55 years old, and neither of you may be under 19 to take advantage of the offer.

Sun City West, with about 18,000 residents, is located 14 miles outside of Phoenix. Here the vacation special gives you a week in a furnished garden apartment, the use of the facilities, which include five 18-hole golf courses, and a tour of the community. For this you pay, for two people, $199 plus tax from May 1 through September 30, $299 from October 1 through December 31, and $450 from January 1 through April 30.

Sun City Tucson, eight miles north of the city at the foot of the Catalina Mountains, is a smaller version planned for 5,000 residents, with a desert golf course. Rates are the same.

Sun City Las Vegas, 12 miles out of the city, puts two of you up at Marriott's Residence Inn, a block from The Strip, for six nights and seven days for $399 to introduce you to the community. Here the perks are a free round of golf and lunch for two, daily continental breakfast, a

hospitality hour every weekday evening, your own kitchen, and free airport shuttle.
For information: Sun City West: 1-800-528-2604. Sun City Tucson: 1-800-433-9611. Sun City Las Vegas: 1-800-843-4848.

UNIVERSITY BRITAIN
A traveler any age, including yours, gets bed and full English breakfast for $30 a night ($28 if you mention this book) in residence halls in any of 17 universities throughout Britain. These include London and eight other city and country campus locations in England, eight in Scotland, and two in Wales, all available during July, August, and September as well as during Easter and Christmas vacation periods. You may stay for as many nights as you wish, usually in a single room, but sometimes twin rooms are available.
For information: Campus Holidays USA, 242 Bellevue Ave., Upper Montclair, NJ 07043; 1-800-526-2915.

Chapter Twelve
Perks in Parks and Other Good News

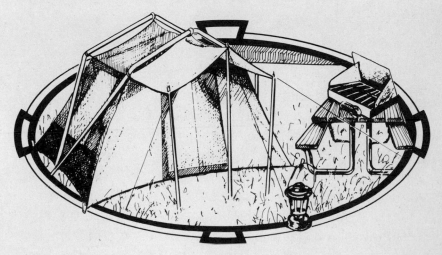

Here and there throughout the United States and Canada, clever states, provinces, and cities have thought up some enticing ideas designed to capture the imagination of people on the other side of 50. Often they are expressing their appreciation of our many contributions to society and simply want to do something nice for us. And sometimes they are trying to lure a few of our vacation dollars to their vicinity, having discovered that we're always out for a good time and know a nice deal when we see one.

But, first, keep in mind:

▶ Before you set forth to visit a new state, it's a good idea to write ahead for free maps, calendars of events, booklets describing sites and scenes of interest, accommodation guides, and perhaps even a list of special discounts or other good things that are available to you as a person in your prime.

▶ Many states offer passes to their state parks and recreation facilities free or at reduced prices to people who are old enough to treat them properly.

After the section on national parks, state park passes and other notable deals are described under each state on the following pages. There may be other good deals that have escaped our attention, but those in this chapter are probably the cream of the crop.

NATIONAL PARKS

GOLDEN AGE PASSPORT

Available to anyone over 62, this is a free lifetime entrance permit to all of the federal government's parks, monuments, and recreation areas that charge entrance fees. Anybody who accompanies you in the same non-commercial vehicle also gets in free. If you turn up at the gate in a commercial vehicle such as a bus, the passport admits you and your spouse, your children, and your parents too, so remember to take them along.

You will also get a 50 percent discount on federal use fees charged for facilities and services such as camping, boat launching, parking, cave tours, etc.

The passport is not available by mail. You must pick one up in person at any National Park System area where entrance fees are charged or at any National Park Service and Forest Service headquarters or regional office, most ranger station offices, Fish and Wildlife Service offices, or National Wildlife Refuges. You must have proof of age. A driver's license will do just fine.

(The Golden Access Passport provides the same benefits for the disabled of any age. The Golden Eagle Passport, for those under 62, costs $25 per year.)

For information: National Park Service, PO Box 37127, Washington, DC 20013.

CANADIAN NATIONAL PARKS

All you have to do to get free entry for day visits is to show your driver's license and vehicle registration. The same is generally true for provincial parks, with half-price camping fees charged on the weekends.

STATE OFFERINGS

For a free listing of all the state tourism offices and their toll-free numbers, send a self-addressed, stamped envelope to Discover America, Travel Industry Association of America, 2 Lafayette Center, 1133 21st St. NW, Washington, DC 20036.

CALIFORNIA

Palm Springs' Super Seniors is a package of programs and activities designed specifically for people over 50. You'll need a valid P.S. Pass (a free pass that gives you a few discounts in Palm Springs and Palm Desert; get yours at the Palm Springs Leisure Center) and a nominal fee to join. With a Super Senior stamp on your P.S. Pass card, you'll be in line for a free T-shirt, free admission to a film festival, and discounts on dance lessons, riding lessons, theater admission, ice skating, fitness classes, hikes, dances, and yoga.

For information: Greater Palm Springs Convention and Visitors Bureau, 255 N. El Cielo Rd., Palm Springs, CA 92262-6993; 619-323-8272.

Senior Season at San Francisco's Pier 39 runs from November 1 to March 31. If you are 55 or over, you're eligible for a Senior Season Savingsbook that includes coupons for discounts at shops, restaurants, and attractions, plus a chance to win a monthly drawing for a two-night free stay in a downtown hotel. Write for the Savingsbook or pick one up at the San Francisco Experience.

For information: Pier 39, PO Box 3730, San Francisco, CA 94119; 1-800-325-7437 or, in California, 415-981-8030.

COLORADO
The Aspen Leaf Pass entitles Colorado citizens 62 and over to free entrance to state facilities and free camping on weekdays.

For information: Colorado Tourism Board, 1625 Broadway, Denver, CO 80202; 303-592-5410.

FLORIDA
Orlando/Orange County has its own version of coupon books to entice visitors to the area in the fall. Once offered only to older tourists, now it is available to anyone. The coupons are good for savings on assorted purchases from hotels and motels to lobster dinners.

For information: For a free copy of the *Fall Celebration Coupon Book*, write to Orlando/Orange County Convention and Visitors Bureau, 7680 Republic Dr., Orlando, FL 32819; 305-345-8882.

INDIANA
The Golden Age Pass for those over 60 admits the bearer and all fellow passengers in a private vehicle to all Department of Natural Resources properties. The pass costs $5 a year.

United Senior Action is a statewide political action organization whose primary purpose is to promote legislation and other measures that help older people. In addition to its lobbying function, it has developed a package of benefits for its members, including a prescription drug program, legal services (free consultation with a lawyer plus answers to legal questions), a consumer handbook, and some discounts.

For information: United Senior Action Foundation, 6940 E. 38th St., Indianapolis, IN 46226.

GOOD NEWS FOR RVers

Safari Campgrounds and **Yogi Bear Jellystone Camp Resorts** will give you, if you're 60, a 15 percent discount on daily site rental fees at their participating campgrounds sprinkled around the United States and Canada. To get it, you must have an SC identification card. Buy a card when you next stop at a campground or send for it.

For information: Send $2 and proof of age (make a photocopy of your driver's license) to Leisure Systems, 14 S. Third Ave., Sturgeon Bay, WI 54235; 1-800-358-9165.

Cruise America, which rents motor homes and vans, will deduct 10 percent from your bill if you flash your AARP card, proving that you are 50 or more. Advance reservations are necessary.

For information: Call 1-800-327-7778 (in Canada and Alaska, 1-800-327-7799).

Some **KOA Kampgrounds** will give you a discount simply because you've joined a 50-plus organization, but most don't—which is OK, because all you need is the KOA Value Card, and that's available to everyone. It will get you 10 percent off the regular registration fees at participating locations. It costs $6 and is available at Kampgrounds or by mail.

For information: Send $6 to KOA Value Card, PO Box 30558 VCD, Billings, MT 59114.

P.S. If you travel solo in your RV, check out Loners of America and Loners on Wheels in Chapter 6.

NEW YORK

Simply by proving you are a New York resident and are over 62 with your driver's license or a state ID card, you will get all the privileges that used to be yours with New York State's Golden Park Pass. You have free vehicle access to state parks and recreational facilities, free admission to state historic sites and arboretums, and a 50 percent reduction on some park activity fees such as swimming and golf. Available on weekdays, no holidays. **For information:** Call 518-474-0456 or your county Office for the Aging.

OHIO

Residents of Ohio who are 60 or over may get a Golden Buckeye Card for the asking. The Card will get them discounts on goods and services from participating businesses throughout the state.

For information: Contact your local Golden Buckeye coordinator for sign-up sites or write to Golden Buckeye Program, Ohio Commission on Aging, 50 W. Broad St., Columbus, OH 43266; 614-466-3681.

TENNESSEE

Travelers over 55 can find bargains in the state of Tennessee every September, generally from Labor Day to the end of the month. The Senior Class gives you discounts of at least 10 percent on hotels and motels, attractions, restaurants, and retail shops. You'll also get 20 percent off on lodging and camping in state parks most of the year and 10 percent from May 1 through Labor Day with a federal Golden Age Passport. **For information:** Tennessee Department of Tourist Development, PO Box 23170, Nashville, TN 37202; 615-741-2158.

UTAH

The Silver Card issued by Park City is a summer program of discounts in this old mining town that's known for its great ski mountains. About 40 restaurants and retailers participate in giving older visitors discounts on their wares. To go along with the shopping and eating possibilities, Park City also presents a whole schedule of activities designed especially for the mature crowd.

For information: Park City Area Visitors Bureau, 528 Main St., Park City, UT 84060; 1-800-453-1360 or 801-649-6100.

The Good Sam Club is an international organization of RVers, mentioned here because the vast majority of people in rolling homes are over 50. This club can be very handy and reassuring when you're cruising the country. Among its benefits are 10 percent discounts on fees at thousands of campgrounds and on propane gas, RV parts and accessories; in addition, it offers a lost-key service, lost-pet service, trip routing, mail-forwarding service, telephone-message service, a magazine, caravan gatherings, and campground directories. Probably the most important benefit is the emergency road service available to members because it includes towing for any vehicle, no matter how large. That's hard to get. Also, there are Good Sam travel tours all over the world, many of them "caraventures." And not least, about 2,200 local chapters hold regular outings, meetings, and campouts. Membership costs $19 a year per family.

For information: The Good Sam Club, PO Box 500, Agoura, CA 91301; 1-800-234-3450.

VERMONT

Vermont's residents over 60 can purchase a Green Mountain Passport for $2 from their own town clerk. It is good for a lifetime and entitles them to free day-use admission at any Vermont State Park and its programs. Other benefits include discounts on concerts, restaurant meals, prescriptions, etc.

VIRGINIA

Williamsburg makes September a special season for people over 55, with more than 80 local businesses offering special discounts and rates (up to 25 percent off) at hotels, motels, guest homes, attractions, restaurants, campgrounds, shops, golf courses, car rentals, tours, and more.

Everybody goes here primarily to visit 18th-century Colonial Williamsburg, Busch Gardens, the historic villages of Jamestown and Yorktown, and the James River Plantations, but there are many other fascinating places, all of them discounted in September. In addition, special events are planned for every day of the month: arts and crafts fairs, concerts, jazz ensembles, plays, tours, hot-air balloon demonstrations, a Scottish festival, lectures.

Your driver's license will do as ID.

For information: Williamsburg Area Tourism and Conference Bureau, PO Box GB, 901 Richmond Rd., Williamsburg, VA 23187; 1-800-368-6511 (in Virginia, 804-253-0192).

WASHINGTON, DC

The Golden Washingtonian Club is a discount program in the nation's capital for people over 60. With proof of age, both residents and visitors can get discounts from about 1,500 merchants listed in a directory called *Gold Mine*, which is free at many hotels or at the Washington Tourist Information Center. More than 70 hotels offer 10 to 40 percent off regular rates, 80 restaurants take 5 to 20 percent off meals, and many retail stores take 5 to 25 percent off purchases.

By the way, remember the Metro System Family/Tourist Pass in Washington, DC. For $5, this gives up to four people unlimited travel on Metrobus and Metrorail for an entire day (on Saturday, Sunday, and federal holidays). Get the pass at your hotel.

For information: Washington Tourist Information Center, 1400 Pennsylvania Ave. NW, Washington, DC 20005; 202-466-GOLD.

WEST VIRGINIA

Everybody who turns 60 in West Virginia gets a Golden Mountaineer Discount Card, which entitles the bearer to discounts from more than 3,500 participating merchants and professionals in the state and a few outside of it. If you don't receive a card automatically, you may apply for one. Flash it wherever you go and save a bundle.

For information: Call 1-800-225-5982 (in Charleston, 304-348-3317).

Chapter Thirteen
Good Deals for Good Sports

R eal sports never give up their sneakers. If you've been a physically active sort all your life, you're certainly not going to be a couch potato now. Especially since you've probably got more time, energy, and maybe funds than you ever had before to enjoy athletic activities and since you may now take advantage of some enticing special privileges and adventures.

The choices outlined here are not for people whose interest in sports is limited to slouching in comfortable armchairs in front of television sets and watching a football game, or settling down on a hard bench in a stadium with a can of beer, yelling, "Come on, team!" They are for peppy people who do the running themselves.

SPORTING GROUPS

NATIONAL SENIOR SPORTS ASSOCIATION
This nonprofit organization has worthy objectives, such as helping you, a sportive person who is over 50, meet new friends and "maintain and improve physical and emotional health through active sports participation."

The NSSA organizes recreational and competitive

tournaments in golf, tennis, bowling, skiing, and fishing at resorts around the country, and arranges sports-oriented trips abroad at special group rates. Last year, for example, there were NSSA events in Acapulco, Las Vegas, Myrtle Beach, Hawaii, Ireland, and Palm Springs, among other choice spots.

Membership—which costs $25 for one year, $65 for three years, $150 for life—entitles you to participate in the sports events and trips and also:

▶ Get discounts on sports equipment, apparel, publications, and leisure products
▶ Travel overseas to play golf or tennis at international resorts
▶ Receive a monthly newsletter
▶ Enter contests and buy sports books at discounts
▶ Send for names and addresses of members so you can get together for friendly matches when you're traveling on your own

For information: NSSA, 10560 Main St., Suite 205, Fairfax, VA 22030; 703-385-7540.

MT. ROBSON ADVENTURE HOLIDAYS
Adventurous over-50s are the exclusive participants in this tour operator's special trips that take place several times every summer high in the Canadian Rockies. Among the trips are hiking/canoeing vacations, heli-camping, and heli-hiking, all of which require you to be in good shape, athletic, and game. See Chapter 3 for more details.
For information: Mt. Robson Adventure Holidays, Box 146, Valemount, BC V0E 2Z0, Canada; 604-566-4351.

OUTDOOR ADVENTURES FOR WOMEN OVER 40

Any reader of this book is certainly over 40 and therefore qualifies, if female, for the trips organized by Outdoor Vacations for Women Over 40. Founded in 1983 by Marion Stoddart, an avid outdoorswoman and conservationist who didn't want to hike, bike, camp out, ski, raft, and canoe with women half her age, this organization attracts physically fit adventurers whose ages, to date, have ranged up to 81.

Ms. Stoddart's surveys have found that a little more than half of the participants in her adventure trips are married; about half are employed; the other half are homemakers, retirees, or volunteers. They come from all over the country, though most are from New England, are in good condition, and rate themselves as beginners or intermediates in the activity they're signing up for. They all love the outdoors, or they wouldn't be there.

The trips are led by trained guides and include instruction, lodging, food, transportation. When you're not camping out in tents or under the stars, you'll be staying in first-rate accommodations.

Previous adventures have included a 10-day walking tour in England, a two-week hiking trip in Switzerland and France, a cross-country skiing vacation in Glacier National Park, a canoe trip in Vermont, rafting in Yellowstone. There are also day trips out of the Boston area, doing such things as animal tracking, orienteering, hiking, and canoeing.

For information: Outdoor Vacations for Women Over 40, PO Box 200, Groton, MA 01450; 508-448-3331.

GETTING IN SHAPE
FIT OVER FIFTY

Run by the Institute for Success Over Sixty, the Fit Over Fifty Seminars are action programs held in Aspen, Colorado, and Alta, Utah, in summer and winter. The six-day summer seminars take you hiking in the mountains and rafting on the rivers, and provide morning sessions on such subjects as health and nutrition, physical fitness, personal development, and relationships. The winter seminars offer instructions and analysis of performance in both downhill and cross-country skiing along with the educational sessions. The package includes lodging, meals, parties.

For information: Fit Over Fifty, PO Box 160, Aspen, CO 81612; 303-925-1900.

THE OVER THE HILL GANG

This international club for energetic people on the far side of 50 began as a ski club (three former Colorado ski instructors were looking for company on the slopes; see Chapter 14), but its members can now be found participating in all kinds of athletic endeavors. Its literature states that it is "an organization for active, fun-loving, adventurous, enthusiastic, young-thinking persons. The only catch is, you have to be 50 or over to join." (Spouses may be younger, however.) You don't have to be a super-jock to be a member, but you do have to like action.

Right now, the club has about 2,500 members and 15 Gangs (chapters) coast to coast (Chicago, Denver, Eastern, Albuquerque, Mt. Hood, Nashville, Rapid City,

Washington, DC, Los Angeles, Orange County, Miami, New England, Reno, San Diego, Southern California). When there's no Gang in your vicinity, you may become a member at large and join in any of the goings-on. These include ski trips, scuba diving, hiking, vacation trips, camping and fishing, ballooning, surfing, canoeing, whatever. Each Gang decides on its own activities. Just plain travel is on the agenda too (see Chapter 3).

The annual fee ($50 single, $80 per couple for a local Gang membership; $25 and $40 for membership at large) gives you a bimonthly newsmagazine, discounts, and a chance to join the fun.

For information: Over the Hill Gang International, 13791 E. Rice Pl., Aurora, CO 80015; 303-699-6404.

BONUSES FOR BIKERS

Biking is becoming one of America's most popular sports, and people who never dreamed they could go much farther than around the block are now pedaling up to 150 miles in a day. That includes over-the-hill bikers beyond 50 as well as youngsters of 16, 39, or 47. In fact, some tours and clubs in the U.S. and Canada are designed especially for over-50s.

AMERICAN YOUTH HOSTEL BIKE TOURS

Although almost every organized biking tour would be delighted to have you along as long as you are fairly adept at pedaling, there's one outfit that's actively looking for you. That's American Youth Hostels, which despite its name sometimes offers bike trips—among other adventure trips (see Chapter 3)—specifically for people over 50. That doesn't mean, of course, that you're not also invited to pedal along on any other adult AYH tour.

You'll stay at hostels that offer simple dormitory-style accommodations, eat local food, and meet people who enjoy doing the same kinds of things you like to do. Trips are limited to groups of 10; all are escorted by trained leaders and are astonishingly inexpensive.

Recent trips offered by AYH exclusively for the mature crowd include cycling in Hawaii and Europe, in New England during the foliage season, and along the Wisconsin Bikeway.

AYH membership, which is required, costs $25 per year unless you're over 55, in which case it's only $15. **For information:** AYH, Dept 855, PO Box 37613, Washington, DC 20013-7613; 202-783-6161.

BACKROADS BICYCLE TOURING

Backroads, an established West Coast biking tour operator, has recently begun offering Prime-Time Tours, special bike trips for people over 50. This year there are two weekend tours in California's Santa Ynez Valley and two week-long trips to Puget Sound. And, of course, you are welcome to join any of the other tours planned for all ages. If you are single, think about one of the 30 bike trips for single travelers in the U.S. and other parts of the world. Trips are rated for Beginners, Energetic Beginners, Intermediates, or Advanced. All tours are led by a guide and accompanied by a van that carries your luggage—and you, if necessary. **For information:** Backroads Bicycle Touring, 1516 5th St., Berkeley, CA 94710; 1-800-533-2573 (in California, 415-527-1555).

BICYCLE TOURING FOR WOMEN ONLY

The same agency mentioned earlier, Outdoor Vacations for Women Over 40, includes a few bike trips among its active offerings. Recently, there was a day trip in southern New Hampshire and Massachusetts, a weekend of biking and walking on Cape Cod, another on Martha's Vineyard and Nantucket, a combination canoe-and-bike trip in Vermont, and a weekend on Block Island in Long Island Sound.

For information: Outdoor Vacations for Women Over 40, PO Box 200, Groton, MA 01450; 508-448-3331.

THE CROSS CANADA CYCLE TOUR SOCIETY

This club was formed in 1982 by a group of "senior cyclists," ranging from about 60 to 75, who biked several thousand miles across Canada in 100 days. Since then, the club has sponsored many cycling trips for all ages and gets local members out for 30- to 50-mile rides twice a week. On the long trips, bikers camp out and make many miles a day. Says the society, "Our aim is to stay alive as long as possible," a worthy goal. Membership costs $20 per year single or $30 per family; most members live in British Columbia.

For information: The Cross Canada Cycle Tour Society, 1200 Hornby St., Vancouver, BC V6Z 2E2, Canada.

ELDERHOSTEL'S INTERNATIONAL BICYCLE TOURS

Elderhostel, famous for its educational travel programs on the campuses of colleges and universities, also offers bicycle tours that combine biking 25 to 35 miles a day with lectures by the historian who accompanies each trip and guests and specialists from other universities. You bike as a group but at your own pace, with regular stops for lectures, site visits, snacking, and relaxing. Bikes are provided, as are breakfast and dinner. Accommodations are in clean, simple, double hotel rooms, most with private baths. A van travels with you to carry the luggage and bike equipment. It will also give you a ride if you think you can't pedal up another hill.

Current trips include 13 days in East Anglia in England, France's Loire Valley, or a lovely area of the Netherlands. The very moderate cost covers airfare and just about everything else except lunches.
For information: Elderhostel, 80 Boylston St., Suite 400, Boston, MA 02116; 617-426-8056.

THE ONTARIO MASTERS CYCLING ASSOCIATION

A biking club with members from all over the Canadian province of Ontario, all of them over 40 and some of them into their high 70s. It is primarily a racing club and organizes 12 events a year within the province, including time trials of 40 and 80 kilometers as well as pursuit and road races of 60 kilometers.

But the club also organizes bike tours for ordinary nonracing persons of both sexes. And you don't even have to be a formal member to join them—just show up at the start and ride. Among its other enticements, there are social get-togethers, a monthly newsletter listing upcoming events, and tips on buying good bikes and finding good meals en route.
For information: Ontario Masters Cycling Association, RR #3, Caledon East, ON L0N 1E0, Canada; 416-880-5136.

THE TANDEM CLUB OF AMERICA

While not strictly for over-50s, the Tandem Club definitely lists many seniors among its members so we are including it here. Founded in 1976 by a group of tandem enthusiasts, the club sends out a newsletter full of arti-

cles and tips about tandems and touring on them, and promotes rallies for owners of the "long bikes." Membership fee is now $10 in the U.S., $13 in Canada.
For information: Tandem Club of America, c/o Boyd and Allison, 19 Lakeside Drive NW, Medford, NJ 08055.

WANDERING WHEELS

A program with a Christian orientation, Wandering Wheels runs long-distance bike tours in this country and abroad, including its 40-day Breakaway Coast-to-Coast for people who are "middle age or older." Its literature says, "The program carries a strong Biblical emphasis."
For information: Wandering Wheels, PO Box 207, Upland, IN, 46989; 317-998-7490.

BICYCLE RACING

Now we're leaving recreational pedaling behind and getting into really serious stuff. So, unless you're a dedicated racer who's in terrific shape, feel free to skip this section.

The United States Cycling Federation, part of the U.S. Olympic Committee, is a racing organization that conducts races for members between the ages of 9 and 89. It's composed of about 800 member clubs throughout the country that promote activities for beginners and run their own races for the more experienced.

Participants in the events must be USCF-licensed riders (this requires a license fee of $32, a completed form, and proof of citizenship and age). Anybody can join. Everyone starts in the entry-level category, then is upgraded appropriately. Riders over the age of 30 are divided into five-year incremental classes and compete against peers. Women do not race against men but form their own age groups.

Members receive a monthly publication that lists the upcoming events. The clubs and local bike shops also can provide information about races.
For information: USCF, 1750 E. Boulder St., Colorado Springs, CO 80909; 303-578-4581.

MORE TIPS FOR BICYCLISTS
The *Tourfinder*, a guide to more than 150 operators who run bicycle tours in the United States and around the world, is available from the League of American Wheelmen. It gives locations, miles covered per day, level of difficulty, prices, accommodations, tour dates, and other information.
For information: League of American Wheelmen, 6707 Whitestone Rd., #209, Baltimore, MD 21207.

TENNIS, ANYONE?

An estimated four million of the nation's tennis players are over 50, with the number increasing every year as more of us decide to forego rocking chairs for a few fast sets on the courts. You need only a court, a racquet, a can of balls, and an opponent to play tennis, but, if you'd like to be competitive or sociable, you may want to get into some senior tournaments.

UNITED STATES TENNIS ASSOCIATION
The USTA offers a wide variety of tournaments for players over the advanced age of 35, at both local and national levels. To participate, you must be a member ($20 per year). When you join, you will become an automatic member of a regional section, receive periodic schedules of USTA-sponsored tournaments and events in your area for which you can sign up, get a discount on tennis books

and publications, and receive a monthly newsletter and a free subscription to *Tennis* magazine.

In the schedule of tournaments, you'll find competitions listed for specific five-year age groups: for men from 35 to 80-plus and for women from 35 to 70-plus. There are also self-rated tournaments that match you up with people of all ages who play at your level. If you feel you're good enough to compete, send for an application and sign up. There is usually a modest fee.

For information: USTA, 707 Alexander Rd., Princeton, NJ 08540; 609-452-2580.

RECREATIONAL SENIOR TENNIS LEAGUE

Because so many mature people play tennis (an estimated 700,000 over age 55), the USTA has come up with an inexpensive kit of material showing you how to launch teams of players of the same level of play in parks, tennis clubs, and community centers.

For information: USTA Center for Education and Recreational Tennis, 707 Alexander Rd., Princeton, NJ 08540.

SENIOR NATIONAL CHAMPIONSHIPS

Also sponsored by the USTA are these tournaments for very serious senior players, who are divided into divisions by gender and age. There are four national tournaments per age group—ages 35 to 75 for women and 35 to 85 for men. Singles, doubles, and mixed doubles tournaments are held on four kinds of surfaces—indoor, grass, clay, and hard courts—at facilities throughout the United States. Added attractions: father-son and mother-daughter doubles events.

For information: USTA Seniors Dept., 1212 Ave. of the Americas, New York, NY 10036; 212-302-3322.

SUPER-SENIOR TENNIS

This group, which has been described as "an affinity group" or a fraternity of male players who compete in the USTA tournaments, promotes tennis for men from 55 to 85 (or more) and arranges a series of tennis events for them in warm places like Florida during the off-season.

"Our members like to compete and to win," says a spokesperson. "Our constant aim is more tournaments for players in the USTA age divisions for men 55 and over. . . . Super Senior tennis players are the last true amateurs in the sport. No one gets paid to play in a tournament, no one receives travel expenses, and we discourage prize money tournaments."

In return for your tax-deductible contribution of $12 a year, you receive a membership card and a bimonthly newsletter that lists tournament dates and results and other matters of interest.

For information: Super-Senior Tennis, PO Box 5165, Charlottesville, VA 22905.

VAN DER MEER TENNIS CENTER

On the resort island of Hilton Head, the center offers a 10 percent discount on its tennis clinics to members of AARP.

For information: Van der Meer Tennis Center, PO Box 5902, Hilton Head Island, SC 29938-5902; 1-800-845-6138 (in South Carolina, 803-785-9602).

MORE TENNIS VACATIONS

If playing tennis is an essential part of a vacation for you, check out the offerings of the National Senior Sports Association and the Over the Hill Gang (see the beginning of this chapter). These groups organize tennis-oriented trips.

HORSEBACK RIDING VACATIONS

FITS EQUESTRIAN

If a horseback vacation is your idea of heaven, look into Fits Equestrian which packages horse tours all over the globe and sets aside five of them a year for people over the age of 60 (or a little below). These special trips "differ from our general rides only in that they are for people wishing to ride at a leisurely pace while enjoying the countryside and that you will be riding with people of your own age group, which often makes for more compatibility." Of course the mixed-age-group rides are also open to you. Recent trips—scheduled from May through September—have been to Argyll, Scotland; Alsace in France; the Black Forest of Germany; Lough Derg, Ireland; and Pleasant River, Maine. Companions who don't ride are free to travel along the same route by car. Riding groups are small and led by a guide.

For information: Fits Equestrian, 60+ Club, 2011 Alamo Pintado Rd., Solvang, CA 93463; 805-688-9494.

MOTORCYCLE HEAVEN

RETREADS MOTORCYCLE CLUB

Retreads are motorcycle enthusiasts who have reached the ripe old age of 40 and who get together to talk cycling mainly through correspondence. Sometimes, though, they meet at area, regional, and international rallies, with or without their bikes. If you join—there is no membership fee—a club newsletter will keep you informed of the activities going on among the 30,000 members in the U.S., Canada, and a few other countries.

For information: Retreads Motorcycle Club International, 8749 SW 21st St., Topeka, KS 66615; 913-478-4508.

CANOE VACATIONS

CANOE COUNTRY ESCAPES

You have to be 50 plus (or go with a companion who has reached that advanced age) to get aboard the Senior Lodge-to-Lodge Trips and Senior Base Camp Packages that take you on wilderness canoe trips in the Minnesota-Ontario Boundary Waters. On the six-day lodge-to-lodge trips out of northeastern Minnesota set for late summer, your nights are spent camping out or staying at rustic fishing lodges, while during the day you paddle the rivers and lakes along the Canadian border. On the wilderness base camp trips you stay at a permanent tent camp in a wilderness area with a cook and a guide, paddling, exploring, fishing, and viewing wildlife on your own schedule. Prior to setting forth the first day of these trips, a guide will conduct a canoe instruction and practice session.

For information: Canoe Country Escapes, 194 S. Franklin St., Denver, CO 80209; 303-722-6482.

WHAT'S GOING ON FOR GOLFERS

GREENS FEES

Most municipal and many private golf courses give senior golfers (usually those over 65) a discount off the regular greens fees. Take your identification with you and always make inquiries before you play.

THE GOLF CARD

This card, designed especially for senior golfers with lots of time to play on every possible golf course, costs $75 the first year for a single membership or $120 for a couple and thereafter $65 single and $105 per couple per year. It entitles you to play two complimentary 18-hole rounds at each of about 1,700 member golf courses throughout the world.

You'll also receive the bimonthly *Golf Traveler* magazine, which contains a directory and guide to the courses and resorts that participate and a travel atlas to help you find them.

Added attraction: Discounts at many resorts when you book golf travel packages.

There is no age minimum for joining this group, but just to give you an idea of its membership: the average member is 61 and has played golf for 24 years, plays 81 rounds a year, travels 11 weeks a year, travels with a spouse, and plans golf as part of his or her leisure travel. **For information**: The Golf Card, 1137 E. 2100 South, PO Box 6439, Salt Lake City, UT 81406; 1-800-453-4260 (in Utah, 801-486-9391; in Canada, 1-800-321-8269).

GOLFING VACATIONS

The National Senior Sports Association (see the beginning of this chapter) organizes many golfing vacations for its members at courses and resorts all over the country and abroad.

SWIMMING FOR FUN AND FITNESS

Swimming, a great way to get exercise and stay in shape, is, for most of us, simply a matter of jumping into the nearest lake or pool and butterflying around, maybe doing a few laps. But if you'd like to be organized about it, you'll find that many Ys and other pool operators have special swim classes or meets for adults. Or you can get really serious and join the Masters Swimmers.

U.S. MASTERS SWIMMING

Originally an organization for young competitive swimmers fresh out of college looking for people to race against, today the Masters is a group that is about 80 percent recreational swimmers, many of whom are over 50. Members get swimming insurance and receive a national newsletter and a magazine that offer information about places to swim, groups to swim with, tips on techniques, and the like. There are 54 local associations across the United States for you to hook up with and several weekend or week-long swim camps to consider.

If you're into competition, at whatever age or level of ability, you may participate in local, regional, and even national meets. Competitors are grouped in heats according to their times, regardless of age or sex. But results are tabulated separately for men and women and in five-year age groups right through 90-plus.

For information: USMS National Office, 2 Peter Ave., Rutland, MA 01543; 508-886-6631.

GETTING INTO THE NATIONAL GAMES

U.S. NATIONAL SENIOR OLYMPICS

Inaugurated at Washington University in St. Louis in the summer of 1987, these Olympic games are a biannual event occurring in the odd-numbered years. Regional Senior Olympic games have been around for over 15 years, but this was the first time a national competition had ever been staged for older athletes who want to win medals for their prowess.

To qualify for the more than 500 separate events—in track and field, swimming, cycling, golf, tennis, bowling, volleyball, horseshoes, archery, 10-kilometer run, badminton, softball, shuffleboard, and table tennis—athletes 55 and up must compete first at sanctioned state and regional Senior Olympics across the country. The events are organized for men and women in five-year age brackets from 55 to 80-plus.

If you want to be ready to go for the next senior games, get the ground rules from your local Senior Olympics organization or the national group.

For information: U.S. National Senior Olympics, 14323 S. Outer Forty Rd., Ste. N300, Chesterfield, MO 63017; 314-878-4900.

STATE SENIOR GAMES

Many states hold their own senior games once a year or so and send their best competitors to national events. If you don't find your state among those listed here, that doesn't mean there's no program in your area—many are sponsored by counties, cities, even local agencies and colleges. Check with your local city, county, or state recreation department to see what's going on near you. You don't have to be a serious competitor to enter the state or local games but merely ready to enjoy yourself. So what if you don't go home with a medal? At the very least, you'll meet other energetic people and have a lot of laughs.

CALIFORNIA

The Southern California Regional Senior Olympics is sponsored by the city of Palm Springs. The first games in 1987 were held over three days and included anyone 55 to 80 (one female swimming contestant was 89) competing in rodeo, ice skating, free-throw shooting, rope skipping, and basketball, as well as all the other sports that could lead to participation in the National Senior Olympics.

For information: Southern California Regional Senior Olympics, Community Services Dept., PO Box 1786, Palm Springs, CA 92263; 619-323-8272.

COLORADO

The Rocky Mountain Senior Games, held in both the summer and the winter, recently celebrated its 10th anniversary. The event is open to residents of Colorado and Wyoming who are 55 and over, with a registration fee of $10. The three-day summer games are held at the University of Northern Colorado in Greeley, Colorado, where you'll pay a minimal fee for lodging, and include such events as track and field, swimming, tennis, basketball, biking, bowling—plus a considerable number of training clinics, workshops, banquets, and dances.

For information: Rocky Mountain Senior Games, 2604 S. Pennsylvania, Denver, CO 80210; 303-777-0471.

The Winter Senior Games, featuring downhill skiing, cross-country skiing, speed and figure skating, a biathlon, and a snowshoeing competition, are usually held in February at a Colorado Ski resort. The small registration fee allows participation in as many events as you wish.

For information: Phyllis Hammond, Blue Cross/Blue Shield of Colorado, 700 Broadway, Denver, CO 80273; 303-831-2216.

CONNECTICUT

The Connecticut Senior Olympics includes not only competitive sport events but also a mini health-fair and physical fitness activities. Connecticut residents and those from neighboring states who are 55-plus converge on the University of Bridgeport on the first Saturday in June for a day of events such as the 5,000-meter run, the 100-yard dash, a mile run, the long jump, diving, bocci, and tennis. There is no entrance fee.

For information: Connecticut Senior Olympics, Harvey Hubbell Gymnasium, University of Bridgeport, Bridgeport, CT 06601.

FLORIDA
The Golden Age Games in Sanford are the biggest and the oldest Senior Games in the country. Held annually in November, they go on for a week and include plenty of competitions, ceremonies, social events, and entertainments. If you are over 55, you are eligible to participate regardless of residency. In other words, you needn't be a Florida resident to compete for the gold, silver, and bronze medals in such sports as basketball, biking, bowling, canoeing, checkers, diving, dance, swimming, tennis, triathlon, track and field, canasta, and croquet. There is a small entry fee for each event.

For information: The Greater Sanford Chamber of Commerce, PO Drawer CC, Sanford, FL 32772-0868; 305-322-2212.

MICHIGAN
Michigan Senior Olympics, a one-day happening open to people over 55, is held in August on the campus of Oakland Community College in Farmington Hills. For small registration and event fees you get lunch and a chance to compete for a medal in athletic events such as discus throwing, 100-yard dash, diving, and cycling. You can also take home ribbons for your superior cookies, cakes, or breads or your prowess at checkers, arts and crafts, and dancing.

For information: Michigan Senior Olympics, O.P.C.,
312 Woodward, Rochester, MI 48063; 313-656-1403.

MISSOURI

The St. Louis Senior Olympics has become an institution
in Missouri by now. A four-day event that is open to
anyone who lives anywhere and is 55 years old, it costs a
nominal amount and is action-oriented. No knitting contests here—only energetic events such as bicycle races,
200-meter races, standing long jumps, tennis singles and
doubles, and swimming.
For information: Senior Olympics, JCAA, 2 Millstone
Campus, St. Louis, MO 63146.

MONTANA

The Big Sky State Games are held each July in Billings,
again for people over 55.
For information: The Big Sky Games, PO Box 2318,
Billings, MT 59101.

NEW YORK

New York Senior Games for state residents over the age
of 55 are usually held on a state college campus over a
weekend in the spring. Competition is divided into age
categories starting with 55 to 59 and going up to 80-plus
with activities ranging from archery and badminton to
cycling, billiards, and volleyball. Also included are a
dinner with entertainment and dancing, workshops, and
clinics—all for a modest fee.
For information: New York Senior Games, State Parks,
Agency 1, 12th Fl., Albany, NY 12238; 518-474-2324.

NORTH CAROLINA

After local games held all over the state, the winners of

the North Carolina Senior Games travel to Raleigh for the state finals and/or to the national games. Every sport from billiards to spin casting to track is on the agenda.

For information: North Carolina Senior Games, PO Box 33590, Raleigh, NC 27606; 919-851-5456.

PENNSYLVANIA

The Pennsylvania Senior Games "combines sports, recreation, and entertainment with fellowship." You can get some of each if you are a Pennsylvania resident who is 55 or older. The games are held over four days at a university campus where you can get lodging and three meals a day for remarkably low cost. If you prefer to stay in a motel, you'll get a senior discount.

For information: Pennsylvania Senior Games, 231 State St., Harrisburg, PA 17101-1195.

VERMONT

The Green Mountain Senior Games in Poultney, whose major sponsor is Killington Ski Area, require you to be a Vermont resident who is over 55 and an amateur at your sport. For a small $5 registration fee, you play, eat lunch, and have fun. Competitive events—organized in age groups of 55 to 62, 63 to 70, and 71 and over—include everything from golf and tennis to swimming, darts, horseshoes, walking, running, table tennis, bowling, croquet, softball and shuffleboard. Just for fun, there are folk and square dancing, volleyball, walking, free swims. The games are held in the early fall.

For information: Green Mountain Senior Games, PO Box 1660, Station A, Rutland, VT 05701.

VIRGINIA

Virginia Golden Olympics is a four-day happening in the spring, this one at Lynchburg College, where athletes compete to qualify for the U.S. National Senior Olympics—or just for the fun of it. The event combines social events and entertainment with sports events. The fees are low, lodging and meals are cheap, and the sporting events are many. Some of the more novel competitions include jump rope, miniature golf, riflery, and Frisbee throws along with the usual swimming, tennis, running, and the like, for various age groups from 55 to 85-plus. **For information**: Golden Olympics, PO Box 2774, Lynchburg, VA 24501; 804-847-1640.

WASHINGTON

A truly athletic happening, the Seattle Senior Sports Festival is a Regional Qualifying Event for the national games and involves only serious sports including track and field, tennis, lawn bowling, pickleball, swimming, table tennis, and softball. The small entry fee covers as many sports as you'd like to enter. You are eligible if you are 55 or over and are an amateur in your chosen sport. **For information**: Senior Sports Festival, 100 Dexter Ave. North, Seattle, WA 98109-5199; 206-625-2981.

EVENTS FOR RAPID RUNNERS

MASTERS TRACK & FIELD AND ROAD RACES

Masters are men and women 30 and over who participate in organized track and field meets and road races. There are no qualifications to join. "About all you need is a pair of shorts, a pair of shoes, and an occasional entry fee if you decide to compete in a meet or race," says

National Masters News, a monthly newspaper and the main source of information about events, providing results, schedules, and local information for each region of the country. "Masters competition is divided into 5- or 10-year age groups for men and women. Every event from the 100-yard dash to the shot put to the marathon is available."

If you want to compete after working out on your own or in a club, there are many meets and races with prizes awarded by age categories. For most of them, you simply show up at the right time and place, register, and participate, although you may wish to sign up in advance.

When you're really experienced, you travel to regional, national, and international competitions, where you'll pay your own expenses and compete as an individual. "The championship events are open to everyone," says long-distance running committee chairman Bob Boal.

For information: Masters Long Distance Running, TAC/USA, 4261 S. 184th St., Seattle, WA 98188. To subscribe to the monthly newspaper, write to *National Masters News,* PO Box 5185, Pasadena, CA 91107.

FIFTY-PLUS RUNNERS ASSOCIATION
This is not a club, although it occasionally sponsors over-50 runs. It is an organization that was formed by high-level exercise researchers at Stanford University "to provide a basis for exchanging information about running and its benefits (and hazards) among the obviously large and growing number of over-50 runners. Another objective was to establish a cadre of people who could serve as a basis for studies of the impact of running on many aspects of life."

Its members, who live in almost every state and in

several foreign countries, receive a quarterly newsletter and are asked to participate in ongoing surveys and studies. Members are asked to contribute $10 a year (tax-deductible) to defray costs.

For information: Fifty-Plus Runners Association, PO Box D, Stanford, CA 94305.

FOR OVER-50 SOFTBALL PLAYERS

NATIONAL ASSOCIATION OF SENIOR CITIZEN SOFTBALL

To play ball in one of the teams sponsored by this organization, you must be at least 50, and there's no upper age limit. The NASCS is an association of several thousand teams around the country, with a goal of promoting a worldwide interest in senior softball. It hosts a national tournament every July and puts on yearly exhibition games and tournaments in several foreign countries. A quarterly newsletter keeps members up to date on happenings.

For information: NASCS, PO Box 1085, Mt. Clemens, MI 48046; 313-792-2110 or 313-286-8757.

Chapter Fourteen
Adventures on Skis

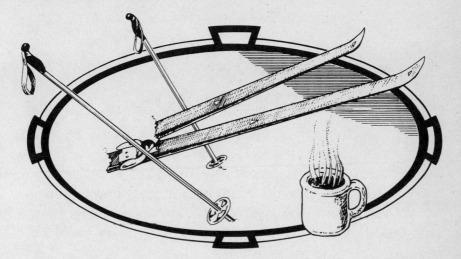

OVER THE TOP ON
TWO NARROW BOARDS

Downhill skiing is one sport you'd think would appeal only to less mature, less wise, less breakable people. On the contrary, there is an astounding number of ardent over-50 skiers who would much rather glide down mountains than sit around waiting for springtime. In fact, many of us ski more than ever now that we're older because we can go midweek when the crowds are thinner. And many of us are taking up the sport for the first time. Ski schools all over the United States and Canada are reporting an increase of older students in beginner classes.

The truth is, skiing is one sport you're never too old to learn or to practice. Once you get the hang of it, you can ski at your own speed, choosing the terrain, the difficulty level, and the challenge. You can swoop down cliffs through narrow icy passes or wend your way down gentle slopes in a more leisurely fashion, aided by the new improved skis and boots, clearly marked and carefully groomed trails, and those newfangled lifts that take all the work out of getting up the mountain.

Besides, ski resorts are falling all over themselves to lure older skiers to their slopes, offering discounts, free passes, and other engaging incentives. Many over-50 groups sponsor ski activities as well.

CLUBS FOR MATURE SKIERS

THE OVER THE HILL GANG

As we have noted, this group originated with a group of older skiers who wanted companionship on the slopes, and skiing is still its main emphasis. In fact, its motto is "Once you're over the hill, you pick up speed!"

If you've hit 50, you are eligible to join (your spouse may be younger) and set forth on ski adventures—both downhill and cross-country—in this country and abroad. Members get discounts on lifts and rentals and sometimes are the recipients of free group guides and special lift-line privileges. People who have never put on a pair of ski boots or haven't tried them in years can take advantage of refresher clinics or group lessons arranged by the club.

And when the ski season ends, you can join the Gang for a bike trip, a party, maybe rafting or ballooning or a sailing trip in the Caribbean. This club, with an age range of 50 to 94 and an average age of 58, is definitely out for fun.

Every year the club organizes a Senior Ski Week in the Rockies or Europe, a package deal that includes accommodations, parties, food, and lift tickets, sometimes lessons. And many members participate in a week of skiing at five different resorts around Lake Tahoe.

The local Gangs also run their own ski trips both in their own vicinities and elsewhere in the world, and all members everywhere are invited to go along. Often there are certain days of the week that the Gangs gather, meeting at a ski area's base lodge and dividing into groups with their own member guides. They rally at reserved spots for lunch, ski some more, then get together for après-ski gatherings and a bit of bragging.

Membership in a local Gang costs $50 ($80 for a couple). If there's no Gang in your vicinity, you may join the national club as an at-large member for $25 ($40 per couple). A quarterly newsletter is part of the deal.
For information: Over the Hill Gang International, 13791 E. Rice Pl., Aurora, CO 80015; 303-699-6404.

70+ SKI CLUB

You have to prove you are 70 before you're invited to join this club, which now has about 4,500 members in their 70s and 80s and a few in their 90s, all of them active downhill skiers. The club meets at various ski areas—usually in New York or New England—for races, companionship, and partying and organizes big trips in the United States and Europe.

Lloyd T. Lambert, a former ski writer who was born in 1901, founded the 70+ Ski Club in 1977 with 34 members. One purpose was to make skiing less expensive for older people on limited retirement incomes. He urged ski areas to let members ski free or at discounts, and his campaign worked. Today most ski areas give us offers we can't refuse. Says Lambert, "We provide inspiration to the 40-year-olds who are about to give up the sport because they think they're getting feeble."

Hunter Mountain in New York's Catskills hosts the club's annual one-day meeting early in March every year. This is when the yearly 70+ Ski Races are held, an event so popular that the contestants are divided into three categories—men 70 to 80, women 70 to 80, and everyone over 80. There are serious slalom races as well as "fun" races with awards for the winners presented at a gala party at the lodge.

Most gatherings of the members take place at ski areas in New England and feature special races and special events, but there are always a couple of week-long ventures to the Alps and the Rockies. And the club has members all over the United States and Canada, even some in Europe.

Club members pay only $5—for life. Proof of your date of birth is required with your application, and you must not apply more than two weeks before your 70th birthday! You'll receive a 70+ Ski Club patch, a membership card, a newsletter, and a list of ski areas throughout the country where you can ski free or at a discount. You can also get a list of members for an additional fee so you can arrange your own companionship if you wish.

For information: Lloyd T. Lambert, 70+ Ski Club, 104 Eastside Dr., Ballston Lake, NY 12019; 518-399-5458.

BROMLEY SENIOR SKIERS CLUB

Free membership in this Bromley Mountain, Vermont, club provides skiers over 65 with half-price lift tickets or a half-price season pass good after January 1, discounts on lift-lesson-equipment packages for family members, and preferred parking. Report to Customer Service with your ID for a club card and a parking permit.

For information: Bromley Mountain, Box 1130, Manchester Center, VT 05255; 802-824-5522.

MOUNT SNOW SENIORSKI

Mount Snow offers a couple of special weeks during December and March to skiers over 50. You'll get a discounted five-day lift ticket (it costs $110 at this writ-

ing) and many other activities. There's a Monday afternoon guided ski tour, a wine-tasting party, an ice cream
social, evening sleigh ride, and races. You also get free
overnight ski storage and a card good for discounts in
shops in the ski area. You'll have your own lounge area in
the Base Lodge to meet each morning for complimentary coffee and donuts.
For information: Mount Snow, VT 05356; 800-444-9404
(in NY, NJ, Canada, and New England states: 802-464-
8501).

STRATTON SENIOR SKIERS ASSOCIATION
Join this Stratton Mountain, Vermont, group for a $35
annual fee. Members 62 through 69 may ski for half
price, and those over 70 may ski free. All may also
participate in a special Senior Day each spring that
includes races and a reception.
For information: Stratton Senior Skiers, Stratton
Mountain, VT 05155; 802-297-2200.

WATERVILLE VALLEY SILVER STREAKS
The Silver Streaks of Waterville Valley, New Hampshire, are members of a no-fee club for skiers who have
reached their 55th birthday (and spouses at any age).
Silver Streakers may buy a midweek lift ticket for $5 off
regular midweek price the first time they ski. On subse-
quent nonholiday midweek visits, the lift ticket is reduced $2 each time until it reaches $12, the price paid
the rest of the season. On Tuesdays and Wednesdays, you
get even more: reserved parking, free coffee and donuts,
warm-up runs with the ski-school instructors, and Silver
Streak NASTAR races. Membership also entitles you to
reduced prices on rentals and class lessons and a one-
third reduction on lodging, also midweek.

For beginners over 55, the resort offers a learn-to-ski package with lifts, ski lesson, and rental equipment, all for $24 a day at this writing.

Members of the 70+ Ski Club—and any other intrepid skiers over 70—ski free midweek.

For information: Waterville Valley Silver Streaks, Waterville Valley, NH 03215; 1-800-468-2553 or 603-236-8371.

THE WILD OLD BUNCH

This merry band of senior skiers who navigate the steep slopes of Alta in Utah is an informal bunch of men and women from Utah and many other states who ski together for fun, welcoming anybody who wants to join them. There are no rules, no designated leaders, no lessons, no regular meetings, and no age restrictions, though most members are well past 50, retired business or professional people. Somewhere between 50 and 100 avid skiers now wear the patch.

The group grows haphazardly as members pick up any stray skiers they find on the slopes, showing them their mountain and passing along their enthusiasm for the steeper trails and the off-trail skiing in Alta's famous powder. Says a spokesperson, Rush Spedden, "If you visit Alta and would like to join in some of the old-fashioned camaraderie of skiing, just look for any of us on the slopes or on the deck of the mid-mountain Alpenglow Inn, where we gather for lunch and tales. Either ski with us or grab a seat for some lively conversation."

Although the bunch isn't sexist, some of the wives prefer to stay on less difficult slopes or to travel the cross-country trails, so they wear "Wild Wives" patches.
For information: Look for the Wild Old Bunch on the slopes, or, if absolutely necessary, contact Rush Sped-

den, 4131 Cumorah Dr., Salt Lake City, UT 84117; 801-278-2283.

MORE DISCOUNTS AND FREEBIES FOR DOWNHILL SKIERS

There's hardly a ski area in the country today that doesn't give mature folks a good deal. Many cut the price of lift tickets in half at age 60, others at 62 or 65, and some stop charging at all when you are 65 or 70.

To give you an idea of what some of the ski areas offer you, here is a short list of possibilities throughout North America. This does not include all areas, of course, so be sure to check out others in locations that interest you. *Always ask* if there is a senior discount before buying your lift ticket.

Proof of age will be required in most cases, so remember to take along some identification that includes your date of birth.

CALIFORNIA
At Mammoth Mountain, there is no charge over 65. Alpine Meadows is half price over 65, no charge at 70.

COLORADO
Among the Colorado ski areas offering discounted lift tickets, some starting at 62 and usually charging nothing at age 70, are Aspen, Snowmass, Buttermilk, Vail, Steamboat, Keystone, Winter Park, Ski Cooper at Leadville, Monarch, Estes Park, Breckinridge, Crested Butte, Telluride, Copper Mountain, Eldora, Loveland,

and Purgatory. In fact, it's a rare ski area that has no senior discounts these days.

In addition, a few areas have instituted special senior ski weeks. For example, Steamboat's Seniors Plus Vacation Week for over-45s is a good deal that includes five days of lessons, lifts, races, meals, and parties. Purgatory now has its SnoMasters Ski Weeks for skiers over 55—choose that package and you get discounts on everything from lift tickets to lodging.

IDAHO
Skiers 65 and over get good discounts at the famous ski resort at Sun Valley.

MAINE
Sunday River Ski Resort in Bethel has a White Caps program for skiers 65 and over. You pay $25 for an all-day lift ticket, three hours of instruction, and lunch. See Other Alpine Adventures for the Elderhostel ski weeks at Sunday River.

MICHIGAN
At Crystal Mountain in Thompsonville, senior skiers—55 and older—get a 50 percent discount on all-day lift tickets, lessons, and rentals, valid anytime. The area's Silver Streak Ski Week, for people over 50, is held in midwinter and includes lodging, unlimited skiing, parties, sing-alongs, races, ski clinic, yoga sessions, and more. Both downhill and cross-country skiing here.

More than 30 ski areas all over Michigan now offer a February week of free lift tickets and/or lessons for skiers over 60.

NEVADA
Lift tickets at Mt. Rose are half price if you're over 65. At Ski Incline, every Wednesday is Senior Social Day for over-55s, when for a small fee, you get skiing, morning coffee, brunch, and speakers.

NEW HAMPSHIRE
At Loon Mountain in Lincoln, those 65 to 70 pay a few dollars less than the other skiers for midweek lift tickets and approximately half for season passes, while those above 70 pay not a cent. Also, see pages 168–169 for information about instant free membership in Waterville Valley's Silver Streaks Club.

NEW YORK
At Gore Mountain in North Creek, you get a junior rate throughout the season if you're over 62, and you'll ski free if you're over 70. Every year, the area hosts a special race day for members of the 70+ Ski Club, with fun races, a giant slalom race, a cocktail party, and an awards banquet.

PENNSYLVANIA
Discounted lift tickets are available for Camelback in Tannersville on midweek nonholidays.

UTAH
Park City and Snow Basin offer 50 percent reductions on lift tickets for people who have made it past 65. The lifts are free at Snowbird and Park City at 70.

VERMONT
Vermont's ski areas are old hands at discounts for mature skiers. Among them:

Stratton Mountain gives you half-price lift tickets if you are 62 to 69 and an even bigger discount when you're 70. And there are additional advantages if you join the Stratton Senior Skiers Association.

At Bolton Valley, skiers 70 and over receive a 50 percent discount on all lift tickets. Bolton also runs a January Senior Week that's inexpensive and fun.

Okemo Mountain: 65 to 69 ski at half price, while over-70s ski free.

Pico: Anyone 65 to 69 is charged half price for lift tickets, ski lessons, and equipment rentals. Members of the 70+ Ski Club ski free on weekdays and for half price on weekends.

Haystack: If you're over 65, you ski free during the week. There's a nominal charge on weekends and holidays.

Mount Snow: Discounted lift tickets for seniors, plus a couple of SeniorSki Weeks scheduled for December and March (see pages 167–168).

Bromley: See page 167 for the Bromley Senior Skiers Club.

Jay Peak offers $5 lift tickets for skiers 65 and over and also sponsors races for the older crowd.

Mad River Glen give seniors over 64 a discounted rate on both day and season passes.

Mt. Mansfield at Stowe discounts lift tickets except during holiday periods if you're 65 to 69 and charges nothing for those over 70.

At Ascutney, those 62 and older are offered a lift ticket for $10 a day. If you're over 70, it's free.

Burke Mountain is always free if you're over 65.

At Maple Valley, skiers 60 to 69 ski at half price every day while those over 70 ski free.

Middlebury Snow Bowl sells a discounted season pass to skiers over 62 and gives free passes to over-70s.

Sugarbush: Here you get a reduced rate from age 65 to 69 and pay nothing at all over 70.

Smuggler's Notch: At 55, you are entitled to $1 off the price of the season pass for every year you have lived. At 65, you may buy lift tickets at half price. At 70, Vermont residents stop paying altogether. Valid every day.

VIRGINIA
At Massanutten Mountain in Harrisonburg, those 65 and over pay about two-thirds of the regular rates for lift tickets and ski rentals.

WYOMING
The Jackson Hole Ski Area gives you half price on one- to five-day lift tickets when you're 65.

OTHER ALPINE ADVENTURES

ELDERHOSTEL DOWNHILL SKIING
The Sunday River Inn in Newry, Maine, was the first Elderhostel campus to offer alpine skiing. The week-long programs available several times during the winter include daily skiing and instruction at Sunday River Ski Resort, plus your choice of courses. These programs, like all the other Elderhostel residence courses, are great bargains. Downhill skiing programs are offered at other ski areas as well.

For information: Elderhostel, 80 Boylston St., Suite 400, Boston, MA 02116; 617-426-8056.

DOWNHILL RACES FOR ALL AGES (YOURS INCLUDED)

NASTAR
NASTAR (National Standard Race) is a ski-racing pro-

gram sponsored by *Ski* magazine for recreational downhill skiers whatever their age, with 5,000 races held in
ski areas all over the United States for medals based on
age, sex, and handicap. The age divisions that apply to
you are the following: men and women 50 to 59, women
60 and over, men 60 to 69, and men 70 and over. You may
race on your own or as part of a participating ski club.

If you want to join in the fun, ask for the NASTAR
Registration Desk at your ski area, fill out the registration card that registers you for the season, pay a fee, and
get a souvenir race bib. Each time you race, your day's
best handicap will automatically be recorded at the
NASTAR Computer Center, where your best three hand-
icaps of the season will be averaged. If you are a winner
in your age group (finalists include 10 men and 10
women from each age category), you will be treated to
an expense-paid trip to the finals.
For information: NASTAR, PO Box 4580, Aspen, CO
81612; 303-925-7864.

UNITED STATES SKI ASSOCIATION ALPINE MASTERS

If you're a good competitive skier, how about signing up
to race in the masters races for older skiers sponsored in
various parts of the country every winter by divisions of
the U.S. Ski Association? You'll be competing against
people your own age. In addition to the races held in the
United States, the International Masters Cup series has
entrants from the U.S. and many European countries. To
be eligible for masters races, skiers must join the U.S.
Ski Association and get a racing license.
For information: United States Ski Association, PO
Box 100, 1500 Kearns Blvd., Park City, UT 84060.

CROSS-COUNTRY SKI ADVENTURES

Many cross-country areas also give senior skiers a break. Always ask about discounts before paying admission.

CROSS-COUNTRY SKI AREAS DIRECTORY

Destinations is a national directory of cross-country ski areas. Regional maps (Northeast, Midwest, Rocky Mountains, West Coast) are also available.

For information: Cross Country Ski Areas of America, RD #2, Bolton Rd., Winchester, NH 03451.

CROSS-COUNTRY VACATIONS FOR WOMEN ONLY

If you're female and 40, you qualify for the ski trips run by Outdoor Vacations for Women over 40, and that should make you very happy. This company offers some pretty exciting adventures and promises you the fellowship of women your own age.

For women who live in the vicinity of Boston, there are one-day cross-country ski clinics designed for beginners and intermediates. A day includes lessons, lunch, and ski touring, all for very little cost. Then there are ski weekends in Vermont where you stay at a cozy inn, take lessons, and ski as far as you want; and recently there were one-week ski trips to Glacier National Park and the White Mountains of New Hampshire.

For information: Outdoor Vacations for Women Over 40, PO Box 200, Groton, MA 01450; 508-448-3331.

ELDERHOSTEL

Elderhostel, known for its low-cost learning vacations for people over 60 (and companions who may be younger) at educational institutions (see Chapter 16), has combined cross-country skiing and winter nature exploration since 1978. For instance, at Craftsbury Center in Craftsbury, Vermont, you can ski on a network of trails, explore the countryside, and take courses. At Frost Valley Environmental Education Center in New York's Catskill Mountains, you can ski and learn on 4,500 acres, while at Old Keystone Village in Colorado you'll intersperse courses in ecology and the history of the Rockies with ski touring at 9,200 feet above sea level. At Las Palomas de Taos, New Mexico, you may alternate ski touring with classes on the foods of the Southwest and the arts of Taos.

For information: Elderhostel, 80 Boylston St., Suite 400, Boston, MA 02116; 617-426-8056.

WATERVILLE VALLEY

Cross-country skiers may join Waterville Valley Silver Streaks Club (see pages 166–167) if they are over 55, applying the membership benefits to the resort's 100-kilometer cross-country center.

For information: Waterville Valley, NH 03215; 1-800-468-2553 or 603-236-8371.

RACES FOR CROSS-COUNTRY SKIERS

To ski in the international races run every year by the World Masters Cross-Country Ski Association, you must be over 30. The competitions are separated into five-year age classes all the way up to 75+, separated also by gender. Participants from all nations are invited, and each country is allowed one scoring A team per class and any number of nonscoring B teams. The championship races are held once a year, in Austria in 1988, Canada in 1989, and Sweden in 1990.

For information: World Masters Cross-Country Ski Association USA, 332 Iowa Ave., PO Box 718, Hayward, WI 54843; 715-634-4891.

Chapter Fifteen

Back to Summer Camp

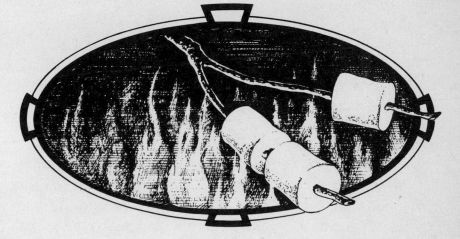

Maybe you thought camp was just for kids, but if you are a grown-up person who likes the outdoors, swimming, boating, birds, and arts and crafts and who appreciates fields and forests and star-filled skies, you too can pack your bags and go off to a "sleepaway." Throughout the country, many camps set aside weeks for adult sessions, while others offer adult programs all season long. More and more adults are getting hooked on summer camp, and many wouldn't miss a year.

ELDERHOSTEL

Many of Elderhostel's programs are a combination of camping and college. In this wildly successful low-cost educational program (see Chapter 16 for details), you can spend a week or two camping in remote scenic areas, enjoying all the activities from horseback riding to crafts, boating, campfires, and sleeping under the stars (or in a cabin). As an example, there are Elderhostel weeks at Classroom of the Earth, affiliated with Colvig Silver Camps, in Red Creek Valley near Durango, Colorado. Most Elderhostel weeks are held, however, on college or university campuses in this country and abroad, where you live in a dorm, eat in the college dining rooms, and take courses in subjects that appeal to you.

For information: Elderhostel, 80 Boylston St., Suite 400, Boston, MA 02116; 617-426-8056.

RV ELDERHOSTELS

Less expensive than regular Elderhostel programs because you take along your own housing, these programs come in two varieties. One is the usual Elderhostel educational vacation on a college campus, where you partake of the happenings, including courses, meals, and excursions, with the rest of the group but sleep in your own RV on the campus or at nearby campgrounds. The other is a mobile program or moving field trip—in Alaska, for example, or Wyoming or along the Oregon Trail—where you'll hear the lectures over your CB radio as you travel.

For information: Elderhostel, 80 Boylston St., Suite 400, Boston, MA 02116; 617-426-8056.

INTERHOSTEL

Sponsored by the University of New Hampshire, Interhostel offers similar arrangements to those of Elderhostel, also inexpensive, but always in foreign countries and for at least two weeks at a stretch (see pages 167–68 in Chapter 16).

For information: Interhostel, University of New Hampshire, 6 Garrison Ave., Durham, NH 03824; 603-862-1147.

GRANDPARENTS CAMP

Every August, you can take your grandchild/grandchildren to camp with you for a week. Designed to help long-distance grandparents get to know their grandchildren and to allow two generations to spend time together free from the restraints of the kids' parents and the responsibilities of everyday life, the camp is sponsored by the Foundation for Grandparenting. The place is Sagamore Institute, a rustic, rambling, nonprofit conference and outdoor recreation center in Raquette Lake, New York, in the Adirondack Mountains. This place was, in a former life, a Vanderbilt family "great camp."

Mornings, children and grandparents engage in joint activities such as walks, hikes, berry-picking, group games, and nature art. Afternoons, each age group is on its own, free to choose from a variety of recreational activities. Before dinner, grandparents get together for discussions on grandparenting issues, and evening sessions again feature togetherness and include such activities as square dancing, stories, campfires, and sing-alongs.

For information: Sagamore Lodge and Conference Center, Sagamore Rd., Raquette Lake, NY 13436; 315-354-5311; or Foundation for Grandparenting, PO Box 97, Jay, NY 12941; 518-946-2177.

THE SALVATION ARMY

The Salvation Army operates 55 rural camps across the country, most of which have year-round adult sessions. The camps are run by regional divisional headquarters of the Army; thus, each is totally different from the others. Open to anyone, they cost very little.

For information: Contact a local unit of the Salvation

Army or write to the national headquarters at 799 Bloomfield Ave., Verona, NJ 07044.

VACATIONS AND
SENIOR CENTERS ASSOCIATION

VASCA is a nonprofit organization that will give you information about camps for people over 55 in the New York area. It represents 17 vacation lodges scattered about New York, New Jersey, Connecticut, and Pennsylvania, most of them for people with an income below a specified level. Some are small rustic wilderness camps, and some are huge sprawling complexes with endless activities. They are sponsored by various nonprofit organizations and foundations, many with religious affiliations, and most are extremely cheap.

For information: VASCA, 275 Seventh Ave., New York, NY 10001; 212-645-6590.

YMCA/YWCA

The Y runs lots of camps, most of them for children, but with special sessions for adults over 50. For example, Westwind on the Pacific is a 500-acre camp owned by the Portland, Oregon, YWCA and located on the coast at the mouth of the Salmon River Estuary. Its senior week, for people over 55, is held every August and costs about $100 for everything. Camp Cheerio, run by the High Point, North Carolina, YMCA, is in the Appalachian Mountains and sets aside three weeks a year for campers over 50, who live in the same cabins and pursue all the same activities as the kids do during the rest of the summer.

For information: Ask your local Y for information about camps in your area.

CAMPS SPONSORED BY CHURCH GROUPS
There are many camps and summer workshops run by church organizations, too many and too diverse to list here. One source of information is Christian Camping International. This organization offers the *Official Guide to Christian Camps and Conference Centers*, which costs a few dollars.
For information: Christian Camping International, PO Box 646, Wheaton, IL 60189; 708-462-0300.

AUDUBON ECOLOGY CAMPS AND WORKSHOPS
Not for over-50s alone, these programs are included here because mature nature freaks will love these natural history programs for adults run by the National Audubon Society. Audubon Ecology Camps are located in Connecticut, Maine, and Wyoming, with sessions from 6 to 12 days. The special workshops include nature photography trips in Yellowstone and Grand Teton national parks and other travel adventures in the Olympic Peninsula, Big Bend National Park in Texas, southern Florida, Arizona, and Costa Rica.
For information: National Audubon Society, 613 Riversville Rd., Greenwich, CT 06831; 203-869-2017.

Chapter Sixteen
Going Back to School After 50

Have you always wanted to learn French, study African birds, examine Eskimo culture, delve into archaeology, international finance, horticulture, the language of whales, or great literature of the 19th century? Now is the time to do it. If you're a typical member of the over-50s generation, you're in good shape, healthy and alert, with the energy and the time to pursue new interests. So why not go back to school and learn all those things you've always wished you knew?

You are welcome as a regular student at just about any institution in the United States and Canada, especially in the continuing-education programs, but many colleges and universities have set up special deals and programs designed to lure older people back to the classroom. Some offer good reductions in tuition (so good indeed that sometimes you may attend classes free) and give credits for life experience. Others have set up programs designed specifically for mature scholars. In some cases, there are whole schools set up just for you.

Going back to class is an excellent way to generate feelings of accomplishment and to exercise the mind—and one of the best ways to make new friends. It doesn't necessarily mean you'll have to turn in term papers or take excruciatingly difficult exams. Sign up for one class a week on flower arranging or Spanish conversation or a once-a-month lecture series on managing your money. Or register as a part-time or full-time student in a traditional university program. Or take a learning vacation on a college campus. Do it *your* way.

You don't even have to attend classes to learn on vacation. You can go on archeological digs, count butterflies, help save turtles from extinction, brush up on your bassoon playing, listen to opera, search for Roman remains in Europe, study dancing or French cuisine, go on safari in Africa.

For a full list of travel study trips around the world, see *Travel and Learn: The New Guide to Educational Travel*, a paperback book that describes more than a thousand vacation programs in the U.S. and abroad offered by 162 universities, colleges, museums, and educational institutions. It will quickly tell you how to find the educational travel programs that appeal to you most. For a copy send $26 (includes shipping) to Blue Penguin Publications, 147 Sylvan Ave., Leonia, NJ 07605.

THE INSTITUTE OF LIFETIME LEARNING

Part of the many services of the American Association of Retired Persons (see Chapter 19), the Institute of Lifetime Learning acts as a clearinghouse and research center on education for older learners and can be a great help in finding out about educational opportunities. Among its most useful offerings is a booklet, *Tuition Policies in Higher Education for Older Adults*, which tells which traditional colleges and universities throughout the country do or do not offer you free or reduced tuition.

Another booklet, *College Centers for Older Learners*,

is a state-by-state listing of learning programs designed specifically for mature students. These range from continuing education to peer-teaching programs.

For information: Institute of Lifetime Learning, 1909 K St. NW, Washington, DC 20049; 202-662-4895.

CAMPUS STUDY/ TRAVEL PROGRAMS

ELDERHOSTEL

Elderhostel, an educational program for older people who want to expand their horizons, offers some of the world's best bargains. Inspired by European hostels and Scandinavian folk schools, it is a network of about 1,000 schools, colleges, and universities in all 50 states, all 10 Canadian provinces, and more than 35 countries overseas, which offer inexpensive short-term residential learning vacations. To qualify, you must be over 60 (or over 50 to accompany someone who is mature enough to enroll).

You live on a campus for a week or more and take up to three courses chosen from a selection of subjects in the liberal arts and sciences taught by the host institution's faculty. These are not for credit, and there are no exams, grades, or required homework; nor must you have any prerequisite knowledge or degrees.

Each institution hosting Elderhostel programs is different in location, size, academic orientation, and atmosphere, and the courses frequently have a regional flavor. The range of courses stretches toward the infinite, an array of impressive proportions, so you are sure to find some that appeal to you. To name a few recent possibilities: Birds of the Southwest, The History of Country

Music, The Rise of Western Civilization, Human Anatomy, Ecology of Alaska, Pollution Alias Self-Destruction, Creative Writing, The Shaker Way of Life, Wines of the World, Vegetarian Garnishes, Appalachian Heritage, the Literature of the Holocaust, and The Art of Weaving.

Most Elderhostel programs are for one week, beginning on a Sunday afternoon and ending the next Saturday morning. You'll sleep in a dormitory. Accommodations vary, ranging from rustic cabins in the Rockies to urban high-rises at city universities. You'll dine on campus food, simple but nourishing, and partake of the school's recreational and cultural resources. The cost for programs in the United States and Canada is remarkably low, usually a little over $200, which covers tuition, room, board, and extracurricular activities. Getting to and from the campus is your responsibility. Many people, incidentally, link Elderhostel weeks, moving from campus to campus for two or three weeks.

The international programs combine morning classes with afternoon excursions, the campus serving as home base as you study the culture, history, and lore of the land with native instructors. These trips cost more, of course, because they usually last three weeks with stays at three different campuses and include land travel as well as airfare from gateway cities.

There is sure to be an Elderhostel program in a place you've always wanted to visit, giving courses you've always wanted to take, at almost any time of the year.

For information: For a free catalogue and other details: Elderhostel, 80 Boylston St., Suite 400, Boston, MA 02116; 617-426-8056. In Canada: Elderhostel Canada, Corbett House, 29 Prince Arthur Ave., Toronto, Canada M5R 1B2.

INTERHOSTEL

An international study-travel program for peppy people over the age of 50, Interhostel is sponsored by the University of New Hampshire. It offers two-week "educational experiences" at colleges and universities in Europe, China, and Australia. The idea is to stay in one place long enough to learn a lot about it, rather than taking a whirlwind tour. So, if you go, you'll come back well acquainted with the country you're visiting. During your stay, you are introduced to its history, culture, and people through a combination of lectures, field trips, and social activities. Your group—limited to 40 people—will be accompanied by a representative of the University of New Hampshire, just to make sure all goes well. The trips are scheduled year-round.

Again, your living quarters—"clean and comfortable, though not necessarily fancy"—will be in residence halls or modest hotels. Most meals are served cafeteria-style and feature the local food of the region. The cost, which is moderate for what you get, includes two weeks' full room and board, tuition, and ground transportation. Round-trip airfare is the least expensive fare available.

Because Interhostel's adventures impose a rigorous schedule of activities and happenings, the agency looks for people who are healthy and fit, full of vim and vigor, and ready to go.

Among the current enticements are two-week trips to England, the Scottish Highlands, Eastern Europe, Ireland, Germany, Puerto Rico, Portugal, Sweden, Switzerland, Spain, China, and more, all of which cost $1,100 to $1,400 plus airfare. Longer adventures to Australia, New Zealand, Thailand, and China cost a bit more.

For information: Interhostel, University of New Hampshire, 6 Garrison Ave., Durham, NH 03824; 1-800-733-

9753 or 603-862-1147, 1:00 P.M. to 4:30 P.M. eastern time.

INTERNATIONAL FRIENDSHIP SERVICE
You can go to college in Europe for intensive instruction in a foreign language (even if you are a beginner) pretty much on a shoestring by signing up for this organization's 1- to 12-week summertime seminars abroad. There are no age limitations—you may be anywhere from 16 to 96, and many of the students are nearing the latter. Current programs are centered at universities in Neuchâtel (Switzerland), Heidelberg (Germany), Cannes (France), Santa Margherita Ligure (Italy), and Corte (Corsica).

What you get at the universities are many hours of French, German, or Italian instruction a week, lodging in student housing or hotel, excursions, tuition, sometimes meals, and other activities. Airfare is not included in the package prices, which are definitely on the moderate side.

For information: International Friendship Service, 22994 El Toro Rd., El Toro, CA 92630; 714-458-8868.

NORTHEASTERN SENIOR SEMINARS
If you're 55 or older, you are eligible to enroll in a series of inexpensive one-week summer residential "campus vacations" at several New York universities. You choose courses from a range of classes from economics to psychology to folk dancing, live in a dorm, and take part in activities on and off campus. There are also commuter and single rates. The schools offering the Senior Seminars are Skidmore College, Long Island University at Southampton, and Ithaca College.

For information: Summer Special Programs, Skidmore College, Saratoga Springs, NY 12866-1632; 518-584-5000.

UNIVERSITY VACATIONS (UNIVAC)
Also for students of all ages, Univac puts you up in a comfortable spacious room for sessions of a week to 12 days in April, July, or August, at either of the two oldest university cities in Europe: Oxford or Cambridge in England. Here mornings are spent attending a series of lectures presented by university scholars, with each session concentrating on a specific subject such as Chaucer's England, the Days of King Arthur and Camelot, Medieval Life, Great Castles and Cathedrals, and the England of Henry James and T. S. Eliot. Afternoons are free for excursions or explorations. Again, the costs aren't likely to break the bank.
For information: Oxford-Cambridge Univac, 9602 N.W. 13th St., Miami, FL 33172; 305-591-1736.

PEER LEARNING PROGRAMS

There are currently about 40 learning programs within colleges and universities throughout the country whose basic concept is peer learning and teaching. This means that classes are led by members, rather than paid faculty, who have special expertise in the subject at hand. The study groups take the form of discussion seminars, lectures, workshops, studio classes, or field trips, with the curriculum planned by the members. In some cases, though not all, members must be retired professionals or executives.

There are no tests or grades, though there may be assigned reading or other preparation, and the plan always includes social activities. Students pay an annual membership fee and may take as many courses as they wish. They also receive student status at the university, giving them all of the usual campus privileges, including the use of the library and the swimming pool.

At many of the schools, you may also take one or two regular undergraduate courses each semester as part of your membership, either without charge or at reduced tuition.

THE INSTITUTE FOR RETIRED PROFESSIONALS

At the New School for Social Research in New York, established in 1962, this was the first such program. As the granddaddy of them all, it has served as a pilot program for similar schools at other institutions. It offers its members—about 650 retired professionals—more than 80 study groups in subjects ranging from Virginia Woolf to Highlights of Mathematics to Bridge for Beginners. Members may also enroll in one regular daytime New School course each semester.

For information: Institute for Retired Professionals, New School for Social Research, 66 W. 12th St., New York, NY 10011; 212-741-5682.

ACADEMY OF LIFELONG LEARNING

For information: University of Delaware, 2800 Pennsylvania Ave., CED, Wilmington, DE 19806; 302-573-4433.

CENTER FOR CREATIVE RETIREMENT

For information: Long Island University, Southampton, NY 11968-4198; 516-283-4000.

CENTER FOR LEARNING IN RETIREMENT

For information: University of California Extension Center, 55 Laguna St., San Francisco, CA 94102; 415-863-4518.

NEVER-TOO-OLD-TO-LEARN DEPARTMENT

SeniorNet started out at the University of San Francisco as a research project to study the use of computer communication networking by people in the over-49 crowd. But it has developed into a club for learners and users of computers. Members may use the equipment at any of the sites throughout the country or join the network via their own computers, modems, software, and phone lines at home.

As a member of SeniorNet, you can send electronic mail to other members; have access to electronic services, programs, and databases; participate in discussions on specific topics; and take part in on-line conferences with the rest of the membership. A manual tells you how to hook up to the network, and a monthly newsletter keeps you up on the latest developments. A membership directory provides information about the interests, expertise, and backgrounds of the rest of the group, allowing you to choose people you'd like to communicate with.

If you live near a SeniorNet site, you can go there for training, networking, and sociability. There are about 30 centers at this writing, and more are in the works.

Annual membership costs $25 and includes the newsletter, the handbook, and a guide that tells you how to connect to the network and make use of its functions. You must pay for your own network time.

For information: SeniorNet, 399 Arguello Blvd., San Francisco, CA 94118; 415-750-5030.

DUKE INSTITUTE FOR LEARNING IN RETIREMENT

Here some of the classes are led by peers, while others are taught by university faculty and local professionals.

For information: Duke University, Durham, NC 27708; 919-684-6259.

THE HARVARD INSTITUTE FOR
LEARNING IN RETIREMENT
For information: Harvard Institute for Learning in Retirement, Lehman Hall B-3, Cambridge, MA 02138; 617-495-4973.

THE INSTITUTE FOR
LEARNING IN RETIREMENT
For information: The American University, Nebraska Hall, 4400 Massachusetts Ave. NW, Washington, DC 20016; 202-885-3920.

A sampling of similar peer learning programs:

INSTITUTE OF NEW DIMENSIONS
Palm Beach Junior College's peer learning school is held at three locations in Florida: Palm Beach Junior College Central Campus in Lake Worth; North Campus in Palm Beach Gardens; and Florida Atlantic University Center in West Palm Beach. Here the yearly fee is very low, and you may take an unlimited number of courses. Student body numbers at about 15,000!
For information: Institute of New Dimensions, Palm Beach Junior College, 3160 PGA Blvd., Palm Beach Gardens, FL 33410; 305-622-2440, ext. 307.

NOVA COLLEGE INSTITUTE FOR
RETIRED PROFESSIONALS
For information: Nova College Institute for Retired Professionals, 3301 College Ave., Fort Lauderdale, FL 33314; 305-475-7036.

THE PLATO SOCIETY OF UCLA
For information: The Plato Society of UCLA, 10995 Le Conte Ave., Los Angeles, CA 90024; 213-825-7917.

PROFESSIONALS AND EXECUTIVES IN RETIREMENT
For information: Hofstra University, 1000 Hempstead Turnpike, Hempstead, NY 11550; 516-560-6919.

TEMPLE ASSOCIATION FOR RETIRED PROFESSIONALS
For information: Temple University, 1619 Walnut St., Philadelphia, PA 19103; 215-787-1505.

MORE GOOD WAYS TO GET SMARTER

CHAUTAUQUA INSTITUTION
The "55 PLUS" Weekends and the Residential Week for Older Adults are sponsored by Chautauqua Institution. For 115 years, people have been going to the shore of Lake Chautauqua, 75 miles south of Buffalo, New York, to a sort of cultural summer camp in a Victorian village. The 856-acre hilltop compound offers a wide variety of programs, including summer weeks and off-season weekends especially for the over-55 crowd. These programs get filled up far in advance, so if you're interested, don't waste a moment.

The weekends each have a specific focus; for example, the U.S. Constitution, natural history, world population, experiencing the arts, trade relations with Japan. They include discussions, workshops, lectures, films, recreational activities, and evening entertainment and are led by professionals. Housing and meals are provided in a residence hall.

The Residential Weeks for Older Adults are similar but longer and include lodging and meals as well as admittance to other goings-on at the center. It's all quite cheap; the current weekly cost of tuition, room, meals, and planned activities for a week amounts to about $265 and for a weekend about $85.

For information: Helen Overs, Program Center of Older Adults, Chautauqua, NY 14722; 716-357-6200.

CLOSE UP

An "educational vacation" in Washington, DC, Close Up is designed for people who are at least 50. The idea is to give you a whole week of firsthand access to "inside" Washington. Activities include two or three seminars a day with key Washington personalities (senators, White House officials, foreign ambassadors, reporters, and others) on topics of current concern; daily briefings for background information; motorcoach tours of the city; a day on Capitol Hill; all meals, many at interesting restaurants; an evening at the theater; daily workshops to discuss issues and events; a banquet; and scheduled free time. You'll lodge in a good hotel.

All this, available to both groups and individuals, is remarkably inexpensive. That's because the weeks are offered in the spring and fall by the Close Up Foundation, a nonprofit, nonpartisan organization that has brought more than 160,000 people of all ages to Washington to study government "on location," in cooperation with the American Association of Retired Persons (AARP).

For information: Close Up Foundation, Dept. POA,

1235 Jefferson Davis Hwy., Arlington, VA 22202; 1-800-232-2000 (in Alaska and Virginia, call collect at 703-892-5428).

THE COLLEGE AT 60
Part of Fordham University and located at the Lincoln Center campus in New York City, the College at 60 offers credit courses in liberal arts subjects such as history, psychology, philosophy, economics, literature, and computers, taught by Fordham faculty members. Included are a lecture series and the use of all college facilities. After taking four seminars, students receive a certificate and are encouraged to enter the regular Fordham University program.

Believe it or not, you are eligible for the College at 60 if you are over 50.

For information: The College at 60, Fordham University at Lincoln Center, 113 W. 60th St., New York, NY 10023; 212-841-5334.

THE EDUCATIONAL NETWORK FOR OLDER ADULTS
This not-for-profit organization in Chicago, which charges nothing for its services, is a network of 65 colleges and universities, adult organizations, community centers, and associations. Its purpose is to help older people in the greater Chicago area find the educational and training programs they need.

ENOA's Resource Center will answer questions on anything "from getting a GED, vocational training and further academic education to finding a bridge group, getting a manuscript published, finding volunteer work, starting a new business, or locating financial-retirement planning seminars." In other words, it's there to help.

For information: The Education Network for Older Adults, 36 S. Wabash, Suite 624, Chicago, IL 60603; 312-782-8967.

THE NEW ENGLAND SENIOR ACADEMY

A weekend residential program, the New England Senior Academy is designed for older people with a love of learning. It is sponsored by the New England Center and the New England Land Grant Universities: University of Connecticut, University of Maine, University of Massachusetts/Amherst, University of New Hampshire, University of Rhode Island, and University of Vermont. The weekend sessions at the New England Center on the campus of the University of New Hampshire begin on Friday evening with a buffet dinner and end with Sunday brunch. Your time is spent in discussions, lectures and demonstrations as well as special events. Each weekend focuses on a specific subject—from art and literature to history and culture—with courses and discussions led by university faculty.

For information: New England Senior Academy, New England Center Program Office, 15 Stafford Ave., University of New Hampshire, Durham, NH 03824-3560; 603-862-1900.

THE NORTH CAROLINA CENTER FOR CREATIVE RETIREMENT

Designed to help the graying set forth on a fulfilling life when they no longer have to spend all their energies on their jobs, this is an unusual setup. For those over 50, it features eight components: a Pre-Retirement Institute to help people make wise decisions about when, where, and how to spend their retirement; the College for Seniors, with a range of courses within the University of North

Carolina, including travel-study courses in many parts of the world; an institute that holds workshops on vital issues such as housing options and finances; a leadership program of accomplished people who provide their expertise to the community and the university; an educational health program; a service league; a council that provides consulting for small businesses; and a research institute. That's a big handful of programs put together for the first time under one umbrella.

For information: The North Carolina Center for Creative Retirement, University of North Carolina at Asheville, Asheville, NC 28804-3299; 704-251-6512.

UNIVERSITY SENIORS

Membership in this New York University program for people over 65 gets you two university courses per semester and biweekly luncheon seminars on subjects of current interest, all for a moderate fee. Recent topics have included U.S. economic power, myths and the Bible, and criminal behavior in America.

For information: University Seniors, NYU School of Continuing Education, 11 W. 42nd St., New York, NY 10036; 212-998-7130.

GETTING AN EDUCATION IN CANADA

Virtually every college and university in Canada offers free tuition to students over the age of 60 or 65, whether they attend classes part-time or full-time. Colleges of applied arts and technology generally offer postsecondary credit courses through their Departments of Continuing Education or Extension to seniors and charge a mere $5 or $10 per course. Aside from the nonexistent or low cost, seniors are treated just like the other students, have the same privileges, and must abide by the same regulations.

For information: Write to the registrar of the college you've chosen for information about its program or, for general information, to the Ministry of Colleges and Universities in your province.

Chapter Seventeen
Shopping Breaks, Taxes, Insurance, and Other Practical Matters

This chapter is not filled with great suggestions for having fun, but the information here may tip you off to some facts and benefits that are coming your way simply because you've lived so long!

SAVING MONEY IN THE STORES

Clever marketing experts have recently realized that the over-50s, a segment now growing three times faster than the rest of the country's population, is the next target market. We not only have more money to spend but are more inclined to spend it than younger consumers. On the other hand, we're a bunch of cautious consumers who know the value of a dollar and are always on the lookout for a bargain.

A couple of large national department store chains offer some special services and enticements to shoppers over 50.

SEARS ROEBUCK & CO.
Sears started Mature Outlook several years ago as an over-50 club. Along with the club's other benefits, it

offers sizable retail price cuts at Sears stores, which members get by cashing in special discount coupons good for a variety of products and services. The coupons come your way regularly once you've joined the organization and may be used in Sears stores in the United States and Canada. See Chapter 19 for the details on signing up with Mature Outlook.

MONTGOMERY WARD
Not to be outdone, Montgomery Ward has started its Y.E.S. (Years of Extra Savings) Discount Club, which aims to save you money in many directions after you hit the magic age of 55. As a member (membership costs $2.90 a month for you and your spouse), you receive a membership card, a Y.E.S. Discount Pass, and a bimonthly magazine called *Vantage*. With the membership card and the pass in hand, you will get 10 percent off any merchandise (sale or non-sale) in Montgomery Ward stores every Tuesday. And, on Tuesdays, Wednesdays, and Thursdays, you will be entitled to 10 percent off auto service.

In addition, the club's Y.E.S. Discount Club Travel Service plans your travel and makes reservations and, on many trips, gives you cash rebates. You also get discounts on car rentals and campground sites.
For information: Montgomery Ward Y.E.S. Discount Club, 200 N. Martingale Rd., Schaumburg, IL 60194; 1-800-421-5396.

FEDERAL INCOME TAX

The most recent tax law does not provide an extra exemption for those over 65 years of age. Instead, it gives you a larger standard deduction than younger people are entitled to, according to Richard Feuerstein, New York accountant. The standard deductions on the short income-tax form for everyone *under* 65 are $5,000 for married couples filing jointly, $2,500 each for married people filing separately, $3,000 for single people, and $4,400 for single heads of households.

However, if one spouse of a couple filing jointly is over 65, the standard deduction is now increased (by $600) to $5,600; if both are over 65, it is increased (by $600 twice) to $6,200. For a married person filing separately, the deduction has increased (by $600) to $3,100. A single person over 65 may now deduct $3,750 ($750 more than those who are younger); and a head of a household's deduction is increased (by $750) to $5,150. None of this applies, of course, if you itemize your deductions.

SALE OF PRINCIPAL RESIDENCE

You can save money on taxes if you are (or your spouse is) 55 when you sell the home you have owned and lived in as a principal residence for at least three years out of the five-year period ending on the date of the sale. You may elect to exclude from your gross income for federal tax purposes up to $62,500 if you are married and filing separately or $125,000 if you are single or married and filing a joint return.

Before you decide to take advantage of this, however, be sure to discuss it with a tax consultant because this exclusion may be used only once in your lifetime and you may be better off saving the privilege for a later home sale.

GETTING HELP WITH YOUR TAX RETURN

Tax assistance is usually available to you free through the Internal Revenue Service or other private and public organizations. Check your telephone book for the appropriate addresses and telephone numbers. Or call your local tax department.

Better yet, contact the Tax-Aide service provided by American Association of Retired Persons (see Chapter 19) which now has thousands of sites around the country where volunteer tax counselors help low- and moderate-income taxpayers over 60 to complete their forms. Watch your local newspaper for the office nearest you or write to Tax-Aide Section, AARP, 1909 K St. NW, Washington, DC 20049.

A NEW LEASH ON LIFE

Through **Purina Pets for People**, an ingenious program funded by Ralston Purina, local humane organizations provide pets for people over 60 at no initial cost to the recipients. The program pays for adoption fees, initial veterinary visits, spaying or neutering, and a starter kit of pet supplies, and contributes a supply of Purina Dog Chow or Cat Chow pet food. The program is designed to rescue a passel of homeless pets, a lot of them grown and trained, and give them to people who'd like the company. Of course, prospective owners must pass their local shelter's screening procedure to be sure they can provide the proper care.

For information: Purina Pets for People, Checkerboard Sq., 6T, St. Louis, MO 63164.

AUTO AND HOMEOWNER'S INSURANCE

Mature people tend to be good drivers, becoming a much better risk class as a group than the younger crowd. You tend to be more careful drivers, having shed most of your hot-rod habits by now, and drive fewer miles. Therefore, statistically, you have about 10 percent fewer accidents per year than other risk categories do. These are the reasons many insurance companies offer discounts on your automobile coverage once you've reached a certain age.

Some companies even offer reductions in premiums for homeowner's insurance as well, figuring you have become a more cautious and reliable sort who takes good care of your property.

Although discounts are wonderful and we all love to get them, they are not the whole picture, according to consumer advocate Robert Hunter of The National Insurance Consumers Organization: "You should shop the bottom line rather than discounts alone, always considering what you pay for the coverage you get. If a company charges higher premiums than other companies for comparable coverage and then gives you a discount, you haven't profited at all. Go for the bottom line with a reputable company."

Because insurance regulations differ from state to state, a complete list of companies giving discounts for age is impossible to assemble. It is best to go through an insurance agent or your state's insurance department. The following, however, are some of the special offerings of major firms in many states.

AETNA

In most states, Aetna gives a discount of about 10 percent off the premium on liability and collision coverage to good drivers 55 to 64 and about 20 percent to those over 65. And, over 55, you also get approximately 40 percent off on comprehensive auto coverage (fire and theft). Driving must be for pleasure use only.

HOW TO SAVE YOUR LIFE

If you happen to have the misfortune of falling ill or having an accident while you're away from home, **MedicAlert** may save your health—or even your life. When you join this nonprofit foundation (lifetime membership costs $25), you receive a metal bracelet or neck chain engraved with your personal identification number and a 24-hour-a-day call-collect telephone number tied into a data bank in California. When you or medical personnel call the data bank, all of your backup medical information is provided along with names and telephone numbers of your physician, next of kin, people to notify in an emergency, and other relevant information. As a backup, you get a wallet card containing the same material.

If you want your bracelet or neck chain in gold or silver, membership will cost you more.

For information: To register by credit card, call 1-800-ID-ALERT. Or write to MedicAlert Foundation, PO Box 1009, Turlock, CA 95381.

ALLSTATE

Allstate gives a 10 percent discount across the board—for all coverage—on both auto and homeowner's policies to people who are at least 55 and retired.

CHUBB

Chubb's offer is 10 percent off for drivers over 50 on liability and collision coverage and a 20 percent discount on comprehensive. Cars must be used for pleasure only, and there may be no youthful drivers (under 25) in the household.

GEICO

Good drivers from ages 50 to 65, using their cars for pleasure only, are given a Prime Time Rating and a discounted premium. Over 65, you're back where you started, however. Homeowners over 50 and retired get a 10 percent discount.

COLONIAL PENN

This company gives a retirement discount if you use your car only for pleasure.

HARTFORD

The company that services American Association of Retired Persons (see Chapter 19) offers members of this organization a discount of about 10 percent for completing an accredited defensive-driving course and up to 10 percent for maintaining a safe driving record. There are also lifetime renewal agreements, credits for low annual mileage, and full 12-month policies.

On homeowner's insurance, Hartford/AARP offers 5 percent credit on your total premium at any age in most states if you are retired.

LIBERTY MUTUAL

Special discounted rates are given by Liberty Mutual across the board on automobile insurance for those over 65.

NATIONWIDE
Nationwide gives a discount of 10 percent on all automobile coverage for people 55 and over.

US F & G
This company offers a discount of approximately 10 percent on auto coverage for people over 65.

BANKING

Many banks offer special incentives and services to people over 55 or 60, ranging from free checking to free NOW accounts, elimination of savings-account fees, free insurance, travelers cheques, and safe-deposit boxes, and even cash rebates at restaurants. Every bank and every state is different, so you must check out the situation in your community. Do some careful comparison shopping to make sure you are getting the best deal available.

LEGAL ASSISTANCE

Call upon your local area senior agency, which is required by law to provide some legal assistance to older citizens. Yours may help you untangle some puzzling legal problems or, at least, tell you what services are available to you. Or contact the local bar association for information. It is quite possible that it operates a referral or pro bono program. Or, suggests the American Bar Association, ask your local Legal Services Program for help or referrals.

NATIONAL RETIREMENT CONCEPTS

If you're thinking of retiring in the Sunbelt, how will you decide where to live? To help you scout a variety of adult communities, National Retirement Concepts takes you on one-week "retirement rehearsal tours" in five states—Arizona, Florida, Arkansas, North Carolina, and South Carolina. You'll talk to local residents, real estate agents, and businesspeople, visit model homes in many developments, and ask all the questions you want. At the same time, you'll see the sights of the area.

For information: National Retirement Concept, Lampert Tours, 1454 N. Wieland Ct., Chicago, IL 60610; 312-951-2866.

Chapter Eighteen
Volunteer for
Great Experiences

There's no need to hang around letting your talents and abilities go to waste once you've quit working for a living. If, perhaps for the first time in your life, you now have hours to spare, maybe you'd like to spend some of them volunteering your services to good causes. There is plenty of work waiting for you. You can find it on your own, of course, but it may be simpler to use the resources of the many programs that are designed specifically to take advantage of your wisdom and experience.

But, first, keep in mind:

Remember, when you file your federal income tax, you are allowed to deduct unreimbursed expenses incurred while volunteering your services. These include transportation, parking, tolls, meals and lodging (in some cases), and uniforms.

The following programs and organizations are actively looking for you and will make a match between you and those who need your help.

RETIRED SENIOR VOLUNTEER PROGRAM
Part of the government's national volunteer agency AC-TION, RSVP serves as a referral and placement service, matching people over 60 with appropriate volunteer work. Operating through local nonprofit private organizations or public agencies, RSVP is tailor-made for each community. In other words, whatever needs doing in your neighborhood is what you'll have a chance to do. You may choose hotlines; provide counseling on drug abuse, nutrition, finances, taxes, home repairs, or wills; or work in crime prevention, home care, or support groups.
For information: Contact your local or regional RSVP or ACTION office or ACTION, 806 Connecticut Ave. NW, Washington, DC 20525; 202-634-9355.

KNITTERS, STITCHERS, AND CARVERS, UNITE!

Elder Craftsmen encourages and advises people over 55 who want to make and sell their own handcrafts. A nonprofit organization operating for more than 30 years, it runs a retail shop in New York that sells most handwork on consignment, with 60 percent of the price going to the artist. Sometimes, however, it provides patterns and materials to skilled workers who work at home to produce specific items in quantity, in which case the craftspeople are paid by the piece. It also offers training courses for representatives of agencies and community groups and serves as an advisory group when needed.
For information: The Elder Craftsmen, Inc., 135 E. 65th St., New York, NY 10021; 212-861-5260.

THE SERVICE CORPS OF
RETIRED EXECUTIVES

SCORE—which now includes ACE (Active Corps of Executives)—is a national organization of both active and retired professionals and business executives who offer their expertise free of charge to small businesses. SCORE counselors, who include lawyers, business executives, accountants, engineers, managers, journalists, and other specialists, provide management assistance and advice to small-business people who are going into business or who are already in business but need expert help.

With a current membership of more than 12,000 men and women, SCORE has about 400 chapters all over the mainland United States as well as Puerto Rico, Guam, and the Virgin Islands. Funded and coordinated by the government's Small Business Administration, it is operated and administered by its own elected officials.

For information: Contact your local U.S. Small Business Administration office or SCORE, 1129 20th St. NW, Suite 410, Washington, DC 20036; 202-653-6279.

AARP VOLUNTEER TALENT BANK

This public service was organized by AARP, the vast over-50 club (see Chapter 19), to help those who wish to serve others. Says a spokesperson, "People over 50 have a lifetime of experience and skills which can apply to a variety of volunteer interests," and the Talent Bank puts people and work together. After you complete a questionnaire about your personal background, interests, and skills, the information is matched by computer with opportunities for volunteer work within American Association of Retired Persons or by referral to other organizations in your own community.

For information: AARP Volunteer Talent Bank, 1909 K St. NW, Washington, DC 20049.

PEACE CORPS
No doubt you've always thought the Peace Corps was reserved for young idealists right out of college. The truth is that it's a viable choice for idealists of any age. There is no upper age limit for acceptance into the Peace Corps, and since its beginning in 1961 thousands of Senior Volunteers have brought their talents and experience to developing countries in Latin America, the Caribbean, Africa, Asia, and the Pacific. To become a Senior Volunteer, you must be a U.S. citizen and meet basic legal and medical criteria. Some assignments require a college or technical-school degree or an experience equivalent. Married couples are eligible and will be assigned together.

What you get in return is the chance to travel, an unforgettable living experience in a foreign land, basic expenses, and housing, plus technical, language, and cultural training. And you will have a chance to use your expertise constructively in fields such as agriculture, engineering, math/science, home economics, education, skilled trades, forestry and fisheries, and community development.

For information: Peace Corps, Room P-301, Washington DC 20526; 1-800-424-8580, ext. 93.

VOLUNTEERS IN TECHNICAL ASSISTANCE
VITA provides another avenue for helping developing countries. A nonprofit international organization, VITA provides volunteer experts who respond—usually by direct correspondence—to technical inquiries from people in these nations who need assistance in such areas as

small-business development, energy applications, agriculture, reforestation, water supply and sanitation, and
low-cost housing. Its volunteers also perform other services such as project planning, translations, publications,
marketing strategies, evaluations, and technical reports
and often become on-site consultants.

There is no minimum age, but you must be retired to
serve. If you become a volunteer, you will not be paid,
but will be reimbursed for your travel and living expenses.
For information: Volunteers in Technical Assistance,
1815 N. Lynn St., Suite 200, Arlington, VA 22209; 703-
276-1800.

FOSTER GRANDPARENTS PROGRAM
This federal program sponsored by the government's
national volunteer agency ACTION offers gratifying volunteer work to thousands of low-income men and women
60 and over, in communities all over the 50 states,
Puerto Rico, Virgin Islands, and the District of Columbia. The volunteers, who receive 40 hours of preservice
orientation and training and four hours a month of in-
service training, work with children who have special
needs—boarder babies; troubled children; handicapped,
severely retarded, abandoned, delinquent, abused, hospi-
talized, addicted, forlorn children who are desperate for
love, care, and attention and do not get it from their
families. They may work in hospitals, schools, homes,
day-care programs, or residential centers.

Volunteers, who must be in good health although they
may be handicapped, work 20 hours a week. For this,
they receive, aside from the immense satisfaction, a

small tax-free annual stipend, a transportation allowance, hot meals while at work, accident and liability insurance, and annual physicals.

For information: Contact your local senior agency or Foster Grandparents Program, ACTION, 806 Connecticut Ave. NW, Washington, DC 20525; 202-634-9355.

JOBS FOR EVERYBODY

If you're still in the market for a paying job, check this organization out.

OPERATION ABLE

If you're over 45 and in the market for a job but don't know where to start looking for one, hook up with ABLE (Ability Based on Long Experience), a nonprofit umbrella organization affiliated with agencies that will match you with a likely employer—that is, if you happen to live in one of the communities where its network of independent agencies performs its magic: Chicago; Boston; Detroit; Los Angeles; New York; San Francisco; Little Rock, Arkansas; Brattleboro, Vermont; and, before long, Lincoln, Nebraska.

ABLE tries every which way to get you into the working world. It provides job counseling, on-the-job training, group training activities, and individual career assessment and guidance; teaches job-hunting skills; matches older workers with employers; operates a pool of temporaries; and offers myriad other services.

For information: Operation ABLE, 36 S. Wabash Ave., Chicago, IL 60603.

FORTY PLUS CLUBS

Offices in 15 cities throughout the United States comprise this nonprofit cooperative of unemployed executives, managers, and professionals, men and women, 40 years of age or more. Their objective is to help members conduct effective job searches and find new jobs. There is no paid staff. The members do all the work and help pay expenses with their one-time charge of $850 (paid in installments). They must commit themselves to attend weekly meetings and spend at least two days a week working at the club and assisting others in their search for work.

In return, members are helped to examine their career skills and define their goals, counseled on résumé writing and interview skills, helped to plan marketing strategy, and given job leads. They may also use the club as a base of operations, with phone answering and mail service, computers, reference library.

Forty Plus Clubs exist at this writing in New York City and Buffalo, New York; Oakland and Los Angeles (with a branch in Laguna Hills), California; Denver (with subsidiaries in Fort Collins and Colorado Springs), Colorado; Chicago, Illinois; Columbus, Ohio; Dallas and Houston, Texas; Salt Lake City, Utah; Philadelphia, Pennsylvania; Washington, DC; and Honolulu, Hawaii.
For information: Addresses of the clubs and descriptive material are available from Forty Plus of New York, 15 Park Row, New York, NY 10038; 212-233-6086.

INTERNATIONAL EXECUTIVE SERVICE CORPS

IESC, organized and directed by U.S. business executives, is a nonprofit organization that recruits retired highly skilled executives and technical advisors to assist businesses in the developing nations. It is funded by the U.S. Agency for International Development (AID), overseas clients and foreign governments, and many American corporations.

After being briefed on the country and the client, volunteer executives travel overseas—with their spouses, if they wish—for projects that generally last two to three months. IESC pays for the couple's travel expenses and provides a per diem allowance.

For information: International Executive Service Corps, 8 Stamford Pl., Stamford, CT 06904-2005; 203-967-6000.

ENVIRONMENTAL PROTECTION AGENCY, SEE PROGRAM

The Senior Environmental Employment (SEE) Program, an EPA-funded project, employs people over 55 part-time or full-time in jobs that help fight environmental pollution. If you sign up, you will be paid an hourly fee not much higher than minimum wage, but, on the other hand, you'll be helping to clean up America.

For information: Contact your regional EPA office or send a letter and résumé to Senior Environmental Employment Program, EPA, 401 M St. SW, Washington, DC, 20460.

NATIONAL EXECUTIVE SERVICE CORPS

This nonprofit organization performs a unique service: it helps other nonprofit organizations solve their problems by providing retired executives with extensive corporate and professional experience to serve as volunteer consultants. Its services are offered in five basic areas—education, health, the arts, social services, and religion—and the assistance covers everything from organizational structure and financial systems to marketing and funding strategy. Volunteers' expenses are covered.

For information: National Executive Service Corps, 257 Park Ave. South, New York, NY 10010; 212-529-6660.

NATIONAL PARK SERVICE

If you love the outdoors and have the time, volunteer to work for the National Park Service as a VIP (Volunteers in Parks). VIPs are not limited to over-50s, but a good portion of them are retired people with time, expertise, talent, and interest in forests and wilderness. You may work a few hours a week or a month, seasonally or full-time, and may or may not—depending on the park—wear a uniform or get reimbursed for out-of-pocket expenses. The job possibilities range from working at an information desk to serving as a guide, maintaining trails, driving a shuttle bus, painting fences, designing computer programs, patrolling trails, making wildlife counts, writing visitor brochures, and preparing park events.

For information: Contact the VIP coordinator at the national park where you would like to volunteer and request an application. Or, for addresses, contact the appropriate National Park Service regional office.

VOLUNTEER PROGRAMS IN ISRAEL

ZOA RETIREES PROGRAM

This is not a tour but a three-month working visit to Israel. You'll be working four hours a day; the rest of the time, you take Hebrew classes, attend a lecture series, tour, visit local homes. To be eligible you must be over 50, physically capable of working at least four hours a day, and in good health. You'll stay in a hotel, get three meals a day, learn Hebrew, and spend 13 days of your time on short trips around the country.

The voluntary work possibilities include tutoring English, providing assistance to aged or ill people, gardening in parks, working at an army base, doing forestry, renovating public buildings, and aiding in hospitals and day-care centers.

For information: ZOA Retirees in Israel Program, 4 E. 34th St., New York, NY 10016; 212-481-1500.

VOLUNTEERS FOR ISRAEL

In this volunteer work-and-cultural program for adults 18 to 69 in Israel you'll put in eight-hour days for three weeks, sleep in a segregated dormitory, and work in small groups at one of 15 army, navy, or air bases, doing whatever needs doing most at that moment. You may serve in supply, warehousing, or maintenance of equipment or in social services in hospitals. You'll wear a uniform with a "Civilian Volunteer" patch. Board and room are free, but you must pay for your own subsidized airfare.

For information: Volunteers for Israel, 330 West 42nd St., New York, NY 10036-6902; 212-643-4848.

ACTIVE RETIREES IN ISRAEL (ARI)

Sponsored by B'nai B'rith International, ARI is a volunteer work program for people who are 50, in good health, and members of B'nai B'rith. Volunteers pay for the opportunity to live in the resort city of Netanya and work in the mornings for two-and-a-half winter months in hospitals, forests, kibbutzim, schools, and facilities for the elderly and the handicapped. Afternoons are spent learning Hebrew, while the evenings include concerts, discussion groups, and cultural activities. Guided tours of the country are part of the program.

For information: ARI, B'nai B'rith Israel Commission, 1640 Rhode Island Ave. NW, Washington, DC 20036; 202-857-6580.

JNF ISRAEL WORK STUDY PROGRAM
In this program sponsored by the Jewish National Fund, you'll spend two or three months in Israel working five mornings a week, learning Hebrew, touring the small desert country, and learning the culture. You must be over 50 and in good enough shape to work hard. You'll have a choice of jobs—some volunteers choose to work in the forests, some in the schools, hospitals, homes for the aged, at army bases, universities, kibbutzim, or perhaps with local craftspeople or archaeologists. Afternoons are devoted to planned activities and evenings to socializing. Included are five days of touring and a month in Jerusalem. The cost is all-inclusive.

For information: JNF Israel Work-Study Program, Migvan Events, 43 W. 33rd St., New York, NY 10001; 212-971-4004.

Chapter Nineteen

The Over-50 Organizations and What They Can Do for You

When you consider that there are more people in this country over the age of 55 than there are children in elementary and high schools, you can see why we have powerful potential to influence what goes on around here. As the "demographic discovery of the decade," a group that controls most of the nation's disposable income, we've become an enormous marketing target. And, just like any other group of people, we've got plenty of needs.

A number of organizations in the United States and Canada have been formed in the last few years to act as advocates for the over-50 crowd and to offer us special deals and services. Here is a brief rundown on them and what they have to offer you. You may want to join more than one of them so you can reap the benefits of each.

THE AMERICAN ASSOCIATION OF RETIRED PERSONS

The biggest, oldest, and best known of all such organizations is AARP, a huge club with a vast array of services and programs. With about 28 million members (6,000 join every day), AARP is open to anyone anywhere in the world who's over 50, retired or not, and so it wields amazing power in the marketplace and among the nation's policy makers. Only two national magazines go to more people than its bimonthly *Modern Maturity*.

For a yearly membership fee of $5 (and that includes a spouse), AARP offers so many things that you are likely to stop reading before you get to the end of the list. But here they are:

▶ Supplemental health insurance at group rates provided by Prudential. All members are guaranteed eligibility.

▶ A nonprofit, mail-order pharmacy service, the largest in the world, that delivers by mail.

▶ Discounts at major hotel and motel chains and resorts and on auto rentals from Avis, Thrifty, Hertz, and National rental agencies.

▶ A money fund in government-backed securities and six mutual funds.

▶ A travel service that offers preplanned tours, cruises, special-event programs "around the world or around the corner," and hosted living abroad, designed especially for mature voyagers (see Chapter 5).

▶ A specially priced motoring plan, provided by Amoco Motor Club, that gets you emergency road and towing service, trip planning, and other benefits.

▶ Auto and homeowner's insurance, via the Hartford Insurance Group, at a discount.

▶ *Modern Maturity* magazine, a bimonthly, full of general articles and useful information, plus a monthly news bulletin.

▶ A national advocacy and lobbying program to develop legislative objectives and priorities and represent the interests of older people at all levels of government, plus volunteer legislative committees that are active in every state.

▶ More than 3,700 local chapters with a range of activities and volunteer projects, from teaching to helping out at the polls.

▶ Volunteer-staffed programs such as tax-preparation assistance, driver retraining, widowed-persons counseling, and Medicare assistance.

▶ Special service programs in such areas as consumer affairs, legal counseling, tax information, housing and health advocacy, women's activities, and crime reduction.

▶ The Institute of Lifetime Learning, a national clearinghouse for educational programs for mature people (see Chapter 16).

▶ Free publications on a large number of subjects relevant to your life.

▶ And even more.

For information: AARP, 1909 K St. NW, Washington, DC 20049.

MATURE OUTLOOK

Only a few years old, this membership organization has already attracted almost a million dues-paying members in the United States. Sponsored by Sears, the country's largest retailer, this club specializes in discounts, some of them hefty, on products and services in its stores, plus many other benefits for people over 50. The annual fee of $9.95, which includes your spouse, also gets you discounts on everything from travel to hotels and motels, used cars, prescriptions, eyeglasses, and lube jobs on your car.

Here's a quick look at this club's services and benefits:

▶ *Mature Outlook Magazine*, which you get every other month. This is a readable, colorful, artfully designed magazine with articles and columns full of information you can use.

▶ *Mature Outlook Newsletter*, which you receive in the alternating months, also a source of useful facts and tips.

▶ Discount coupons from Sears that give you savings on both regular and sale-priced items. The coupons are inside each issue of the newsletter.

▶ Travel Alert (see Chapter 5) for domestic and international tours, cruises, and trips available at big savings because they represent last-minute unsold space and cancellations.

▶ Discounts of 20 percent on the room rates and 10 percent on meals and gifts, at participating Holiday Inns and Crowne Plaza Hotels. Also discounts on car rentals from Budget/Sears, Hertz, Avis, and National.

▶ Mail-order pharmacy discounts, discounts on eyeglasses, and no-fee traveler's checks with home delivery.

▶ A 10 percent discount on every meal you and a guest eat at Holiday Inn restaurants.

▶ A members-only discount on Allstate Motor Club membership.

For information: Mature Outlook, 6001 N. Clark St., Chicago, IL 60660-9977; 1-800-336-6330.

CANADIAN ASSOCIATION OF RETIRED PERSONS

For a few dollars a year you and your spouse can join CARP, a brand-new nonprofit association for Canadians

over 50 (who make up almost a quarter of the country's population). Inspired by AARP, it provides you with discount rates on lots of good things, from health insurance to car rentals, hotels, theaters, and travel. It also sends you a quarterly newspaper called *CARP News*.
For information: CARP, 27 Queen St. East, Suite 304, Toronto, ON M5C 2M6, Canada; 416-363-8748.

CATHOLIC GOLDEN AGE
A Catholic nonprofit organization that is concerned with issues affecting older citizens, such as health care costs, housing, and social security benefits, the CGA has well over a million members and more than 200 chapters throughout the country. It offers many good things to its members who must be over 50. These include spiritual benefits such as masses and prayers throughout the world and practical benefits as well. Among them are discounts on hotels, motels, and campground sites, car rentals, prescriptions, eyeglasses. Other benefits include group insurance plans, pilgrimage and group travel programs, and an automobile club. Membership costs $7 a year.
For information: Catholic Golden Age, 400 Lackawanna Ave., Scranton, PA 18503; 1-800-233-4697.

NATIONAL COUNCIL OF SENIOR CITIZENS
An advocacy organization, NCSC lobbies on the local, state, and national level for legislation benefiting older Americans. With about 4.5 million members, it has carried on many successful campaigns in the areas of housing, health care, Social Security, and the like.

Although NCSC's major focus is its legislative program, it also has a local club network, social events, prescription discounts, group rates on supplemental health insurance, automobile insurance, and travel discounts, plus a newspaper that keeps you up to date on all of the above.

For information: National Council of Senior Citizens, 925 15th St. NW, Washington, DC 20005; 202-347-8800.

NATIONAL ASSOCIATION FOR RETIRED CREDIT UNION PEOPLE

Obviously, not everybody can join this club, but those who can get some good benefits. These include an attractive and useful magazine called *Prime Times* and the *NARCUP Newsletter*, car-rental discounts, Medicare-supplement insurance, pharmacy discounts, lodging discounts at some hotels and campgrounds, and a motor club. Also, discounted travel packages and tours.

For information: NARCUP, PO Box 391, Madison, WI 53701; 608-238-4286.

NATIONAL ASSOCIATION OF RETIRED FEDERAL EMPLOYEES

As you have probably gathered, this is an association of federal retirees and families. Its primary mission is to protect the earned benefits of retired federal employees via its lobbying program in Washington.

For information: NARFE, 1533 New Hampshire Ave. NW, Washington, DC 20036; 202-234-0832.

OLDER WOMEN'S LEAGUE

The league is an advocacy group that works to improve the lot of older women in this country—not an easy job. Through a national organization and local chapters, it provides educational materials, training for citizen advocates, informational publications and the like, dealing with the important issues facing women as they grow older.

For information: Older Women's League, 730 11th St. NW, Suite 300, Washington, DC 20001; 202-783-6686.

NATIONAL ALLIANCE OF SENIOR CITIZENS

This national lobbying organization with more than two million members has a decidedly conservative tilt-to-the-right bias, so people with middle-of-the-road or liberal views would not feel too much at home here. It works to influence national policy "on key issues of great importance to America and her future." As a member you receive newsletters and benefits that include group insurance, prescription discounts, discounts on car rentals, lodgings, moving expenses, and an automobile club.

For information: National Alliance of Senior Citizens, 2525 Wilson Blvd., Arlington, VA 22201; 703-528-4380.

GRAY PANTHERS

With about 40,000 members of all ages, the Gray Panthers fight ageism and speak up for older Americans, reminding people "that people over 65 will not be pushed around by the Administration, not by callous landlords, not by nursing home profiteers, and not by an indifferent health care system. . . . Yet citizens past 65 are consistently the largest and most active voting block in the United States." Major areas of concern include Social Security, housing, nursing homes, Medicare, attitudes.

For information: Gray Panthers, 311 S. Juniper St., Philadelphia, PA 19107; 215-545-6555.

THE RETIRED OFFICERS ASSOCIATION

This group is open to anyone who has been a commissioned or warrant officer in the seven U.S. uniformed services. These folks receive a magazine whose articles are devoted to matters of special interest to them, and lobbying representation on Capitol Hill. They may also take advantage of several benefits, including discounts on car rentals and motel lodgings, a travel program with "military fares" to many overseas destinations, sports tournaments, a mail-order prescription program, group health and life insurance plans, and a car lease-purchase plan. TROA also has many autonomous local chapters with their own activities and membership fees.

For information: The Retired Officers Association, 201 N. Washington St., Alexandria, VA 22314-2529; 703-549-2311.

Chapter Twenty

Practical Reading for People in Their Prime

To keep current on the latest opportunities for good deals and great adventures designed specifically for the mature set, you should do some reading. The following are some publications that consider you their audience. In them, you will certainly find news you can use and information that will be helpful in many areas of your life.

NEWSLETTERS

AARP News Bulletin is part of the AARP package, and you will get it regularly once you become a member. It alerts you to political issues affecting older Americans and to the organization's current benefits and offers, and gives handy tips and pertinent news. Contact AARP, 1909 K St. NW, Washington, DC 20049.

Mature Outlook Newsletter, a lively 16-page publication, is issued six times a year and sent to you when you join Mature Outlook. It is full of news, helpful advice, recommendations, and just plain interesting information about all manner of things. Contact Mature Outlook, 6001 N. Clark St., Chicago, IL 60660-9977; 1-800-336-6330.

The Mature Traveler, a monthly newsletter, aims at providing expert advice on saving money and avoiding trouble when you travel. It will keep you *au courant* on the latest travel offerings and current bargains for "older Americans." Order from GEM Publishing, PO Box 50820, Reno, NV 89513; 702-786-7419.

The Retirement Letter is a monthly publication on making and saving money after you have retired. It is full of useful tips and suggestions that you are sure to profit from. Order from Peter A. Dickinson, Editor, 44 Wildwood Dr., Prescott, AZ 86301.

Travel 50 & Beyond is a new four-color magazine just launched in 1990. It targets leisure travelers in the 50-plus age group and focuses on practical travel information, vacation ideas, health and safety issues, special events, and various kinds of travel from freighter cruises to winter getaways. Contact *Travel 50 & Beyond*, Vacation Publications, 2411 Fountain View, Houston, TX 77057.

Travel Smart is not for mature travelers alone, but its purpose is to help its readers save money when they travel. In it, you will find many ways to do so, and always included are the latest special offers for people over 50. This newsletter makes a point of tipping you off to discounts, unusual travel ideas, and "deals of the month," sometimes special for its readers. For information about subscribing, contact Travel Smart, 40 Beechdale Rd., Dobbs Ferry, NY 10522.

Vital Connections, a quarterly newsletter put out by the Foundation for Grandparenting, works to "encourage understanding between the generations and enrich family connections." Membership in the organization (for a minimum $20 tax-deductible contribution) entitles you to an annual subscription to the newsletter. For details, contact Foundation for Grandparenting, PO Box 97, Jay, NY 12941; 518-946-2177.

MAGAZINES

Golden Years Magazine is a Florida publication that's gone national. It's distributed in supermarkets, drugstores, and banks, or sold by subscription. It tells you what's doing for your age group and how to take advantage of it. It also features general-interest articles on such subjects as travel, health, and real estate. Contact *Golden Years Magazine*, PO Box 537, Melbourne, FL 32902-0537.

Lear's, edited for sophisticated, educated, affluent women over 40, is a new addition to the list of magazines for the older crowd. Available on the newsstand and by subscription, it is a very slick and elegant publication with articles and columns about health, mind, sexuality, finance, work, relationships, fashion, beauty, and the American scene. Contact *Lear's*, 655 Madison Ave., New York, NY 10021.

Mature Outlook, too, is a genuine consumer magazine that is good reading. Part and parcel of your membership in the Sears organization for over-50s and paid for by your yearly dues, its columns on money, health, gardening, and its articles on everything you might want to know about make it a valuable monthly arrival. See Chapter 19 for information about joining the organization and thereby getting the magazine.

Meridian, a magazine for Canadians who are 55 plus, is sent free to any Canadian who requests it (although there may soon be a subscription charge) and costs $10 a year for Americans. Its articles and editorial content are aimed at your age group. Contact *Meridian*, Troika Publishing Inc., Box 13337, Kanata, ON K2K 1X5, Canada.

Modern Maturity is the official AARP magazine, again part of your membership, paid for by your $5-a-year dues and sent to you regularly. This is a real magazine, with general articles, advertising, and columns, as well as information about AARP's many benefits and services. You will find lots to interest you here. See Chapter 19 for information about joining AARP.

New Choices, published by *Reader's Digest*, is a general monthly magazine for an older audience, filled with articles of special interest to seniors. A well-edited publication, it is available on the newsstands and by subscription. *New Choices* will not only entertain you but will provide you with much useful information. Contact *New Choices*, 28 W. 23 St., New York, NY 10010.

Prime Times is a real magazine, a good one, although it is published for the members of the National Association of Retired Credit Union People, which means most people haven't heard of it. It is a topical magazine with broad general appeal. As a nonmember of the sponsoring organization, you may subscribe anyway. Contact *Prime Times*, Box 391, 5910 Mineral Point Rd., Madison, WI 53701.

Index

Running, 159–61
RVs, 18
  discounts, 132
  Good Sam Club, 134
  solo traveling, 63–64

Sabena, 83
Saga Holidays, 20, 38–39, 61
Sagamore Institute, 182
Sailing, 16
Salvation Army, 182–83
San Juan Mountains, 13
Sandman Hotels and Inns,
  111–12
SAS (Scandanavian Airlines),
  83
Scandinavian countries, 31
  air travel, 83
  discounts, 31
  railroad travel, 31
Scandinavian National Tourist
  Office, 31
SCI/National Retirees of
  America, 45
Scottish Inns. *See* Red Carpet
  Inns
Sea Escape Cruise Lines, 48
Sears Roebuck & Co., 38,
  204–5
Senior Escorted Tours, 45
Senior olympics, 153–59
  California, 154–55
  Colorado, 153
  Connecticut, 155–56
  Florida, 156–57
  Michigan, 156–57
  Missouri, 157
  Montana, 157
  New York, 157
  North Carolina, 157–58
  Pennsylvania, 158

Vermont, 158
Virginia, 159
Washington, 159
Senior organizations, 228–32.
  *See also individual
  organizations*
Senior Travel Exchange
  Program (STEP), 18–19
Senior Vacation Hotels of
  Florida, 122
SeniorNet, 194
Seniors
  discretionary income, 8
  domestic travel, 8
  education, 3
  resources, 3
Seniors Abroad, 122–23
Servas, 123
Service Corps of Retired
  Executives (SCORE), 216
70 Ski Club, 166–67
Sheraton Hotels, 112
Shoney's Inn, 112
Shopping, 9, 204–5
Singleworld, 48–49, 61
Ski magazine, 175
Skiing, cross-country, 176–78
Skiing, downhill, 17, 168–77
  California, 170
  Colorado, 170–61
  Idaho, 171
  Michigan, 171
  Nevada, 172
  New Hampshire, 168–69, 172
  New York, 172
  Pennsylvania, 172
  racing, 174–75
  Utah, 169–70, 172
  Vermont, 167–68, 172–74
  Virginia, 174
  Wyoming, 174